The Digital Minimalist's Handbook

A Guide to Simplifying Your Tech Life and Maximizing Productivity

Samantha Keen

Table of Contents

INTRODUCTION

This is "The Digital Minimalist's Handbook: A Guide to Simplifying Your Tech Life and Maximizing Productivity." In the modern world, where technology permeates every aspect of our lives, striking a balance between connectedness and mindfulness is more important than ever. The purpose of this manual is to give people who want to improve productivity, declutter their digital environment, and simplify their connection with helpful technology ideas and insights.

Digital minimalism emphasizes deliberate and thoughtful use of technology rather than open rejection of it. Regaining control over our digital lives is the goal, allowing technology to work for us rather than against us. This book delves into many facets of digital minimalism, including setting limits, handling notifications, organizing a simple digital workspace, and striking a balance between online and outside time.

You will find ideas for assessing your digital habits, reducing distractions, and making the most efficient use of your digital tools in the pages that follow. We examine case studies that demonstrate how digital minimalism affects well-being and productivity, and we offer helpful suggestions on how to put these ideas into practice in your own life.

This book provides a thorough guide to assist you in reaching your goals, whether you're a busy professional trying to optimize your workflow, a student trying to restore focus in a world of continual distraction, or just someone who wants to have a healthier relationship with technology. You can take back control of your time, lower your stress level, and find more balance in your electronic life by embracing simplicity and developing a minimalist mentality.

Come along as we examine the ideas behind digital minimalism and learn how they can improve your relationship with technology. Together, we'll successfully negotiate the challenges of the digital era and equip ourselves to lead more purposeful, effective, and conscious lives in our tech-dependent society.

CHAPTER I

Understanding Digital Minimalism

Introduction to digital minimalism

A contemporary method of handling technology that places an emphasis on intentionality and simplicity is called digital minimalism. In order to improve our productivity and well-being, entails carefully selecting the digital tools, platforms, and material we interact with. Digital minimalism is a means of regaining control over our attention, lowering stress levels, and concentrating on what really matters in a world where digital noise and continual connectivity are ubiquitous.

Less is more is the fundamental tenet of digital minimalism. By making the deliberate decision to reduce our use of and interactions with technology, we make room for other enjoyable and significant pursuits. This strategy focuses on using technology in a way that is consistent with our beliefs and objectives rather than altogether rejecting it. It calls on us to evaluate our use of digital tools critically, consider their purpose, and make deliberate choices about how they fit into our daily lives.

The decrease in digital clutter is one of the main advantages of digital minimalism. An excessive number of apps, files, and notifications are frequently present on our smartphones, which can be distracting and overwhelming. We can make our digital spaces less chaotic and more ordered by clearing them out. This may entail removing pointless apps, arranging files neatly into directories, and controlling alerts to reduce disruptions. Increased productivity and focus can result from a cleaner digital environment.

Setting limits on our usage of technology is another recommendation made by digital minimalism. It is simple to be caught up in the trap of always being connected because digital content and communication are always available. Establishing limits, such as specific times for social media or email checks, can help us take back control of our time and attention. By establishing these limits, we can avoid the frequent task switching that digital distractions frequently bring about and instead fully participate in both our work and personal lives.

The focus on deliberate consumption is another essential component of digital minimalism. We have an endless supply of entertainment and information available to us in the digital age, most of which can be consumed carelessly. We are encouraged by digital minimalism to choose the stuff we interact with more carefully. This entails selecting valuable, high-quality stuff that enhances our lives as opposed to being just time wasters. We can make sure that our screen time is productive and beneficial by being deliberate about what we consume online.

The goal of digital minimalism is to promote a positive interaction between humans and technology. Many of us have made it a habit to check our phones frequently or to aimlessly browse social media. These behaviors may cause tension, anxiety, and unhappiness. We may overcome these patterns and cultivate a more harmonious and constructive connection with technology by taking a minimalist approach. This could entail activities like digital detoxes, in which we purposefully disconnect from technology in order to reestablish relationships with those in our immediate social circles and the real world.

Digital simplicity can increase productivity in addition to enhancing our personal wellbeing. Reducing digital distractions and optimizing our digital tools can help us concentrate better on our assignments and projects. This may result in more productive work and a stronger sense of success. Time-blocking strategies, in which we set aside specific times for various tasks, can assist us in optimizing our time and maintaining focus on our objectives.

Furthermore, digital simplicity inspires us to develop relationships and offline interests. It is simple to overlook in-person relationships and physical activities in a society where technology is everywhere. We may enrich our lives in ways that digital activities cannot by purposefully making time for offline activities. Hobbies, time spent in nature, and fostering relationships with family and friends can offer a sense of contentment and happiness that is sometimes lacking from digital contacts.

Digital minimalism is a technique that is in line with more significant movements that promote purposeful living and mindfulness. It inspires us to enjoy the small things in life and to live in the present. We can improve our awareness of our thoughts, feelings, and environment by cutting back on the electronic world's noise and distractions. There may be an increase in happiness and serenity as a result.

There is no one-size-fits-all solution to digital simplicity. It necessitates that each person consider their own relationship with technology and make modifications based on their tastes and needs. Because of its customized approach, digital minimalism is guaranteed to be adaptive and versatile, making it suitable for a wide range of situations and lifestyles. The concepts of digital minimalism can be adjusted to suit various circumstances and objectives, such as cutting down on screen time, maintaining a simple social media presence, or streamlining digital workflows.

Overcoming FOMO, or the fear of missing out, is one of the problems of digital minimalism. It might be hard to resist the need to stay up-to-date in a society where social media and continual communication are the norm. But digital simplicity shows us that depth, not breadth, is where true fulfillment lies. We can be happier and more satisfied if we concentrate on fewer, more significant events. As we come to understand that we are receiving more by delving deeper into what matters to us, the fear of missing out gradually fades.

The digital minimalism movement has effects on our mental health as well. Persistent exposure to digital content, especially on social media, can cause anxiety, despair, and feelings of inadequacy. We can safeguard our mental health by controlling the stuff we expose ourselves to on digital platforms and avoiding unpleasant or pointless information. By using technology with awareness and purpose, we can build a helpful and encouraging digital environment that improves rather than worsens our mental health.

Furthermore, digital minimalism pushes us to utilize social media more thoughtfully. Social media can be a valuable tool for connecting with people and communicating, but it can also be stressful and a source of distraction. We can minimize the drawbacks of social media while maximizing its advantages by using it thoughtfully and at the correct times. This may be scheduling particular times to check social media, unfollowing accounts that don't make a difference in our lives, and reacting to content more carefully.

Digital simplicity at work can result in more productive and concentrated work habits. Digital tools are necessary for many tasks, but they can also be a source of distraction due to continual notifications. We may create a more focused and effective work environment by implementing digital minimalist principles, such as turning off unnecessary notifications and using productivity tools thoughtfully. This raises our level of performance while lowering stress and increasing job happiness.

Digital minimalism has a place in the classroom as well. Today's students are frequently overloaded with online learning resources and digital content. Technology has the potential to improve education, yet it can also be overpowering and distracting. Students can restrict their exposure to digital distractions and concentrate on top-notch educational resources by taking a minimalist approach. As a result, they may learn more effectively and form better digital habits.

Digital minimalism can help families establish a more harmonious and cohesive home environment. The effects of technology on relationships and everyday routines are a problem for many families. Families may build deeper bonds and more meaningful interactions by establishing rules around technology use, such as dedicated tech-free periods and family dinners without electronics. This can improve harmony at home and strengthen family ties.

There are connections between digital minimalism and the more significant push for sustainability. Digital gadget manufacturing and disposal have a significant influence on the environment. By taking a more simplistic attitude to technology, we may use fewer digital gadgets overall and get more use out of the ones we do. In addition to helping the environment, this also motivates us to make more deliberate and thoughtful purchases.

Digital minimalism has the potential to be a very effective instrument for personal development. We may make more time and space for personal development activities like reading, journaling, and following passions by minimizing digital distractions. A stronger sense of fulfillment and purpose may result from this. We may better connect our digital habits with our long-term objectives by reflecting on our beliefs and priorities, which is another benefit of digital minimalism.

Digital minimalism can also foster our creativity. Constant exposure to digital stimulation can hinder our ability to think deeply and creatively. We can unlock our creative potential by lowering the noise from digital devices and making more room for introspection. This may include making regular tech-free time dedicated to creative endeavors or employing digital tools with greater intention and focus.

Our actual surroundings can also benefit from the digital minimalist tenets. To create a more harmonious and less distracting atmosphere, we can declutter our physical areas in the same way that we do our digital spaces. This all-encompassing method of minimalism can improve our general health and lead to a more contented and balanced existence.

To sum up, digital minimalism provides a method to have a more purposeful, harmonious, and satisfying relationship with technology. Our productivity, general well-being, and overall quality of life can all be improved by clearing out digital clutter, establishing boundaries, and emphasizing conscious consumption. Digital minimalism is about utilizing technology to further our objectives and ideals rather than rejecting it. Digital minimalism offers a vital and refreshing way to manage our online lives in a world where digital noise is everywhere. It pushes us to take it slowly, live in the moment, and concentrate on the essential things. The ideas of digital minimalism can support us in developing a more positive and deliberate connection with technology, whether it be in our personal or professional lives or in educational settings.

Benefits of adopting a digital minimalist lifestyle

Living a digitally minimalist lifestyle has several advantages that can significantly raise one's standard of living. Our relationship with technology can be made simpler, which will improve our physical and mental health, boost productivity, encourage closer relationships with others, and free up more time for worthwhile pursuits. In response to the widespread digital overload that many people encounter today, digital minimalism offers a framework for utilizing technology in a way that is consistent with our objectives and beliefs.

Less stress and anxiety is one of the most significant advantages of digital minimalism. Constant contact and the constant deluge of alerts might lead to a mental health risk of overwhelm and urgency. People can establish boundaries around their technology use by embracing digital minimalism, which contributes to the creation of a more tranquil and orderly atmosphere. The urge to always be available can be reduced by restricting social media use, setting certain times for reading emails, and turning off non-essential notifications. Because there is less digital noise, the mind may relax and heal, which lowers stress and anxiety levels.

Digital simplicity not only lowers stress levels but also dramatically increases concentration and focus. The human brain is not built to withstand repeated disruptions, but contemporary technology demands our attention nonstop. Every alert or signal has the potential to throw off our concentration, making it impossible to work deeply and continuously. Through the reduction of digital distractions, people can create an atmosphere that supports concentrated work. Increased productivity and a stronger sense of achievement may result from this. Our work improves in quality, and we can do more in less time when we can give a task our whole concentration.

Additionally, digital minimalism encourages more profound sleep. The hormone that controls sleep, melatonin, can be produced less effectively by the body in response to blue light provided by screens. Additionally, it may be challenging to unwind before bedtime due to the stimulating nature of digital entertainment. People can enhance the quality of their sleep by cutting back on screen use, particularly in the hours before bedtime. The body can be signaled to relax and get ready for sleep by creating a nightly routine that includes activities like journaling, meditation, or reading a book. Numerous health benefits, such as happier moods, sharper minds, and better immune systems, are attributed to getting enough sleep.

The improvement of interpersonal interactions is one of the main advantages of digital minimalism. Technology can help people communicate, but it can also put up obstacles in the way of sincere human connection. Overuse of digital gadgets can reduce the value of our connections and take away from in-person encounters.

Setting limits on technology use can help people have more opportunities for deep conversations with their loved ones. Deeper relationships can be cultivated and bonds strengthened by partaking in outdoor activities, sharing meals without electronics, or just spending time together without the distraction of screens.

In addition, digital minimalism promotes the pursuit of offline interests and hobbies. A significant portion of leisure time is often spent by many people engaging in digital activities like social media browsing, video watching, or online gaming. Even though these pursuits can be fun, they sometimes don't lead to much personal development or contentment. People can increase their time for happy and fulfilling activities by cutting back on their internet intake. This could include taking up artistic interests, picking up new skills, working out physically, or going outside. Engaging in these pursuits not only offers a feeling of achievement but also enhances general well-being.

Moreover, living a digitally minimalist lifestyle might promote mindfulness and self-awareness. It is simple to go through the motions without really connecting with our thoughts and feelings in a society when digital distractions abound. People who practice digital minimalism are encouraged to live more intentionally and mindfully every day. Making time for introspection and contemplation helps people get a better knowledge of who they are and what they stand for. To strengthen this self-awareness, a digital minimalist lifestyle can benefit from the integration of mindfulness exercises like journaling or meditation. More emotional control, more stress resistance, and a more profound feeling of purpose can result from this increased awareness.

Additionally, digital minimalism can improve physical health. A sedentary lifestyle, which can result in a number of health concerns like obesity, cardiovascular disease, and musculoskeletal disorders, is frequently linked to excessive screen usage. One way for people to increase opportunities for physical activity is by cutting back on screen time. This could be going to the gym on a daily basis, playing sports, or just spending more time outside. Engaging in physical activity enhances one's physical and mental wellbeing simultaneously. It can elevate mood, lessen stress, and boost cognitive performance.

Additionally, there are financial advantages to digital minimalism. There may be pressure to permanently own the newest gadgets and apps because the tech sector is pushed by frequent updates and new releases. People who embrace a minimalistic approach to technology are better able to control their want to upgrade frequently and concentrate on making better use of the gadgets they already have. Over time, this may result in considerable cost savings. Additionally, people can cut back on wasteful spending and improve their financial management by being more deliberate about their online and digital subscription purchases.

The possibility for more creativity is another benefit of digital simplicity. By keeping the mind from roaming and connecting seemingly unrelated ideas, the constant digital stimulus might hinder creativity. People can increase the amount of time they have for creative problem-solving and thought by minimizing digital distractions. The creative process can be sparked by doing things like brainstorming, doodling, or exploring new places. People who practice digital minimalism are more likely to be innovative and creative because they are encouraged to seek out fresh experiences and viewpoints.

Additionally, digital minimalism encourages a more sustainable way of living. Depletion of resources and electronic waste are two significant environmental effects of the creation and disposal of digital gadgets. We can decrease our environmental impact by minimizing the quantity of equipment we own and prolonging the life of the ones we do utilize. We can also lower the energy used by data centers and cloud services by being more conscious of the digital media we consume. Living a more ecologically conscious lifestyle and supporting larger sustainability goals can be achieved by embracing a minimalistic approach to technology.

Digital minimalism has the potential to improve educational outcomes. Digital distractions are a commonplace presence for students nowadays, which can make it difficult for them to focus and remember material. Students' academic performance and study habits can both be enhanced by focusing on the learning environment. This could entail scheduling dedicated study periods, avoiding using electronic gadgets during study sessions, and looking for top-notch learning materials. A more deliberate and focused approach to learning is promoted by digital minimalism, and this can result in improved academic achievement.

Moreover, digital simplicity might strengthen ties to the community. Many people experience feelings of alienation and loneliness in an era where face-to-face communication is frequently replaced by digital connections. People can enhance their social bonds and feel more a part of the community by cutting back on their screen time and giving in-person encounters more importance. Participating in local events, volunteering, and joining clubs and organizations are examples of community activities that might offer possibilities for meaningful social involvement. These relationships improve people's wellbeing on an individual basis as well as strengthen and unite society.

Additionally, digital minimalism promotes a more contented and balanced way of working. The constant barrage of emails, messages, and notifications in many occupations can lead to distraction and a sense of urgency that reduces productivity. Through the implementation of digital minimalism, individuals can establish a work environment that is more efficient and focused. This could entail prioritizing jobs that call for intense concentration, setting aside particular times for checking emails, and shutting off unnecessary notifications. People may operate more effectively and with greater clarity when they minimize digital distractions, which improves performance and job satisfaction.

Furthermore, digital minimalism can improve one's ability to solve problems and make decisions. Making educated decisions might be challenging due to information overload caused by the constant availability of information. We can lessen the cognitive strain brought on by assiduously processing large volumes of information by streamlining our digital lives. This enables us to concentrate on the most pertinent and significant data, which improves our ability to make decisions. Digital minimalism promotes a more cautious and analytical approach to problem-solving, which can enhance our capacity to handle challenging circumstances.

Better time management and efficiency are possible advantages of digital minimalism. Many people discover that they spend more time on digital activities than they think they do, which can take time away from other crucial facets of life. People who embrace a minimalistic approach to technology might increase their awareness of their time management and make more deliberate decisions. This may entail prioritizing activities that are consistent with one's beliefs and objectives, measuring screen time, and establishing clear goals for technology use. Improved time management can result in a life that is more balanced and satisfying.

Additionally, digital minimalism promotes a life that is more purposeful and intentional. It is simple to lose sight of what really matters in a society when digital temptations abound. People can establish a more distinct feeling of purpose and direction by cutting down on digital distractions and concentrating on what matters most. This could entail evaluating one's own values, establishing long-term objectives, and making deliberate decisions that support those objectives. Having a stronger sense of purpose can improve one's motivation, sense of fulfillment, and general well-being.

Moreover, digital minimalism can improve self-control and discipline. Social media and online gaming are two examples of the many digital activities that are made to be highly engaging and can result in compulsive behaviors. People can improve their self-control and self-discipline by taking a more minimalistic approach to technology and their digital habits. This might include establishing tech-free zones, putting screen time limitations in place, or engaging in digital detoxes. Gaining self-control in the digital sphere can help you become more self-aware and evolve as a person in other spheres of life.

Additionally, digital minimalism promotes a deeper awareness of the present. Digital gadgets can constantly divert us from living in the now and savoring it to the fullest. People can develop a stronger sense of thankfulness and appreciation for the present moment by cutting back on their screen time and increasing opportunities for mindfulness and presence. This could entail engaging in activities and conversations while being totally present, as well as mindfulness meditation and nature walks. Happiness and general well-being can rise with a deeper awareness of the present.

Finally, living a digitally minimalistic lifestyle provides a host of advantages that can significantly improve someone's quality of life. Our connection with technology can be made simpler, which will help us focus and concentrate better, feel less stressed and anxious, sleep better, build stronger relationships, and have more time for worthwhile things. Increased intentionality, self- awareness, and mindfulness are encouraged by digital minimalism, which improves wellbeing in general. It promotes improved time management, healthier digital habits, and a more harmonious balance between work and personal life. Furthermore, digital minimalism supports more general objectives like sustainability and community involvement. People can design a more purposeful and fulfilling existence free from the demands and distractions of the digital world by adopting digital minimalism.

Case studies illustrating the impact of digital minimalism

In reaction to the ubiquitous influence of technology in our daily lives, digital minimalism has become a fascinating lifestyle concept. In an effort to lessen distractions and improve productivity, it promotes using digital technologies with intention and mindfulness. This section explores a number of case studies that highlight the significant influence of digital minimalism in several fields, demonstrating the advantages that people, groups, and communities have experienced from implementing this idea.

Cal Newport is a well-known advocate of digital minimalism, and his book "Digital Minimalism: Choosing a Focused Life in a Noisy World" features a ton of case studies. One such case study is on Kieran, a software developer who was preoccupied with electronic devices all the time. Kieran was using his phone for more than five hours every day, which had an impact on both his mental and professional well-being. Kieran chose to practice digital minimalism as a response to his overwhelming sense of overwhelm. He curtailed his usage of non-essential apps and placed stringent boundaries on his digital connections. He switched from mindless browsing to more deliberate pursuits like reading and working out outside. Kieran noticed notable gains in his concentration and mental clarity over time. He saw a reduction in stress and anxiety levels and increased productivity at work.

Digital minimalism has also advanced significantly in the business sector. One noteworthy case study is about Basecamp, an American marketing company. The business understood how destructive continual digital distractions were to workers' well-being and productivity. Basecamp instituted a corporate philosophy that promotes digital minimalism as a means of countering this. By substituting written updates and reports for meetings, they decreased the frequency of meetings and encouraged asynchronous communication. This strategy produced a more productive and contented workforce by allowing workers to concentrate on in-depth work without continual interruptions. Adopting the concepts of digital minimalism resulted in enhanced work-life balance, lower levels of burnout, and higher job satisfaction among employees.

In a similar vein, the German automaker Daimler implemented the "Mail on Holiday" policy to alleviate the anxiety that comes with coming home to a cluttered inbox. When staff are on vacation, this policy automatically deletes any incoming emails, giving them the opportunity to fully unplug and rejuvenate. Employees who returned from holidays feeling more at ease and refreshed saw a significant impact. When they returned to work, their productivity had increased and their well-being had improved since they could finally enjoy their vacation without worrying about an overflowing inbox.

Digital minimalism in teaching has also shown encouraging outcomes. A University of Chicago case study examined how lowering digital distractions affected students' academic performance. A program enabling students to minimize their usage of social media and smartphones during study hours was put in place by the institution. Participants in the program reported increased academic achievement, enhanced focus, and better time management. Many students reported feeling less stressed and anxious because they could focus more intently on their academics without being constantly drawn away by digital distractions. This case study illustrates how digital minimalism in educational settings can have a positive effect on students' learning and well-being.

Reclaiming valuable time together has led families to adopt digital minimalism as well. This idea is demonstrated via a case study on the California Johnson family. The Johnsons observed that their incessant reliance on electronic gadgets was impeding their capacity to foster familial bonds. They made the decision to impose a digital detox policy, setting a daily limit of one hour for screen use and designating weekends as screen-free days. The kids were against the changes at first, but eventually, they warmed up and started to take pleasure in more family chats, board games, and outside activities. The parents said that their relationships with their kids had improved significantly and that they had a stronger bond. They also saw improvements in their kids' sleep and academic performance, proving that digital minimalism has a good effect on family interactions.

Regarding mental health, digital minimalism has demonstrated encouraging outcomes in lowering depressive and isolated sensations. The University of Pennsylvania looked at the impact of reducing social media use on mental health in a case study. For three weeks, study participants were instructed to limit their daily social media use to 30 minutes. The individuals reported notable decreases in their experiences of melancholy and loneliness, which was a noteworthy outcome. People were able to spend less time on social media and increase their offline interactions and interpersonal bonds by participating more deeply in offline activities. This case study demonstrates how encouraging more balanced digital behaviors can help achieve better mental health outcomes through digital minimalism.

Digital minimalism has had a significant influence on artistic endeavors and creativity as well. A case study using writer Emily serves to highlight this idea. Emily discovered that her frequent usage of social media and electronic gadgets was impeding her ability to be creative and productive. By establishing rigorous limits on her technology use and designating specific time for writing without any digital interruptions, she made the decision to embrace digital minimalism. Emily's writing production and quality significantly increased as a result of this transition, which enabled her to reach a state of deep labor. She demonstrated the significant influence of digital minimalism on artistic output when she reported feeling more inspired and involved in her creative process.

Beyond improving one's own well-being, digital minimalism also promotes environmental sustainability. A Swedish software company's case study looked at how cutting back on internet use affected the company's carbon footprint. The business put policies in place to restrict the amount of energy-intensive digital activities, like excessive streaming of videos and cloud storage. Workers were urged to use the ideas of digital minimalism in both their personal and professional lives. Impressively, the company's energy consumption and carbon emissions were significantly reduced. An additional indication of the environmental advantages of digital minimalism is the increased sense of purpose and alignment with the company's sustainability goals provided by employees.

Digital simplicity has been used in the healthcare industry to enhance provider and patient well-being. This idea is demonstrated through a case study involving nurses at a New York hospital. In order to free up nurses' attention for patient care, the hospital instituted a policy limiting digital communications that aren't absolutely necessary during nursing shifts. Nurse burnout was decreased and patient satisfaction levels increased as a result of this adjustment. Adopting the concepts of digital minimalism resulted in nurses reporting feeling more fulfilled in their work and connected to their patients. This case study illustrates how encouraging deeper patient relationships and lowering caregiver stress levels might improve healthcare outcomes through digital simplicity.

Moreover, digital minimalism has demonstrated promise in enhancing collaboration and organizational effectiveness. A Silicon Valley software development company's case study examined the effects of lowering digital distractions on teamwork. The business put in place a policy to restrict digital communications that aren't absolutely necessary and to promote periods of concentrated concentration. Significant improvements in productivity and job satisfaction were reported by the staff. Adopting digital minimalism principles also resulted in a drop in project turnaround times and an increase in innovation for the organization. This case study demonstrates how intentional communication and a decrease in digital noise can promote a more productive and unified work environment through digital minimalism.

To sum up, these case studies demonstrate how digital minimalism can revolutionize a variety of fields. Digital minimalism has shown to be a valuable attitude for managing the difficulties of the digital age, with benefits ranging from boosting individual well-being and productivity to bettering family dynamics, educational outcomes, and environmental sustainability. Digital minimalism is a means to live a more purposeful and happy life by encouraging mindfulness, intentionality, and balance in our interactions with technology. The potential for good will increase as more people, businesses, and communities adopt digital minimalism, paving the way for a time when technology will contribute to rather than take away from human well-being and productivity.

CHAPTER II

Assessing Your Digital Life

Taking stock of your current digital habits

Evaluating your present digital practices entails a thorough and reflective examination of how you use digital gadgets and internet resources on a regular basis. Understanding how these behaviors affect your general well-being, productivity, and social connections requires going through this process. In the digital age, where screens permeate both our personal and professional lives, it is necessary to regularly assess and consider these behaviors to make sure they are consistent with our values and aspirations.

Acknowledging the pervasiveness of digital devices in our lives is the first step towards this assessment. In addition to being tools, laptops, tablets, smartphones, and smartwatches are also extensions of our daily lives and identities. Even before getting out of bed, we check our phones for alarms, jump into a myriad of applications, and browse through social media. Our digital presence frequently eclipses our physical world due to this ongoing connectivity. Thus, assessing our level of digital engagement is the first step towards determining our habits.

An essential component of digital habits is time management. Our productivity and mental health may suffer if we examine the trends in the amount of time we spend on different digital activities. Applications that track screen time can reveal how much time is spent on social media, streaming media, gaming, and other online activities. This information can be eye-opening because it frequently shows that a large percentage of our days are spent passively consuming information as opposed to actively participating in it or working productively. We may start making wise judgments about cutting down on pointless screen time and repurposing that time for other fulfilling pursuits by recognizing these trends.

It is impossible to overestimate the influence of digital habits on mental health. For example, prolonged use of social media has been associated with higher degrees of loneliness, sadness, and anxiety. The culture of comparison that social media sites like Facebook and Instagram promote can cause low self-esteem and feelings of inadequacy. It is critical to consider the impact that our internet connections have on our mental health. Do we use social media to make connections with people or just to measure ourselves against them? Do we read sections that broaden our horizons and deepen our understanding, or do we just aimlessly browse through an endless stream of self-indulgent sections? By addressing these issues, we can develop a more deliberate and attentive attitude toward our use of digital media.

Furthermore, our digital habits have a significant impact on the caliber of our social connections. Our communication has changed as a result of social media and messaging apps' convenience. Even if these tools provide never-before-seen connectedness, they may also result in shallow encounters devoid of emotional resonance. A critical evaluation of our digital communication practices is determining how well we balance our online and offline encounters. Are we using text messaging in place of in-person conversations? At social events, are we attentive and involved, or are we engrossed in our phones all the time? Meaningful relationships require a delicate balance between virtual and in-person encounters.

The impact of digital habits on our work lives is another crucial factor to take into account. With online collaboration, virtual meetings, and remote work becoming commonplace, the modern office is becoming more and more digital. These tools increase productivity and flexibility, but they also make it harder to distinguish between personal and professional life. Setting up limits that are explicit is essential to avoiding burnout and keeping a good work-life balance. Having a dedicated workplace, taking regular screen breaks, and establishing set intervals for reading work emails are all helpful in managing digital work habits.

Our digital habits also include the way we watch and listen to media. There is a vast variety of content available on the internet, including both entertainment and instructive materials. However, the convenience of access may result in a lack of information and short attention spans. Examining the sources of our information and the types of content we interact with is an essential part of reflecting on our habits of content consumption. Are we getting our information from reliable, varied sources, or are we only hearing from voices that confirm our preconceptions? Do we use digital platforms for growth and learning, or are we just using them for mindless amusement to get our fix quickly? Our intellectual and emotional development can be improved by choosing and consuming content with purpose.

Digital habits include not just consuming but also creating and contributing. There is a lot of creative and self-expression potential in the digital realm. The options are numerous, ranging from making music and art to blogging and vlogging. Analyzing our usage of digital tools for self-expression and community participation is part of reflecting on our digital habits. Do we actively create and share content that benefits others, or are we merely passive consumers? Taking part in creative digital activities can enhance one's digital experience by giving one a feeling of purpose and accomplishment.

Another essential factor to think about is the physical effects of digital habits. Extended usage of screens can cause a number of health problems, such as strained eyes, bad posture, and irregular sleep cycles. Examining our ergonomic habits and screen time management is a necessary step in thinking back on our physical relationship with digital gadgets. Do we regularly pause to stretch our muscles and give our eyes a break? Do we use electronics in well-lit areas to lessen eye strain? When using laptops and cellphones, are we keeping our posture correct? Developing safe digital practices can reduce these threats to the body and enhance general wellbeing.

Furthermore, one of the most critical components of our digital behaviors is the digital trail we leave behind. Every action we take online leaves a digital trace that may eventually affect our security and privacy. Evaluating our online sharing habits and privacy settings is part of taking stock of our digital footprint. Do we consider carefully what personal information we provide on social media and other websites? Do we use secure, one-of-a-kind passwords for each of our accounts? Do we know how the websites and apps we use collect and use our data? In an era where cyber-attacks are on the rise, it is imperative that we take proactive measures to protect our digital privacy.

Digital financial practices also need to be considered. While digital subscriptions, in-app purchases, and online shopping have made transactions easier, they can also result in impulsive spending and financial distress. Analyzing our purchasing trends and money management strategies is part of assessing our digital financial habits. Are we monitoring the money we spend on digital products? Do we really use and need the services that we are subscribing to? Do we have spending limits on things we buy online? We may improve our financial health and prevent needless debt by being aware of our digital spending habits.

Another essential factor to consider with digital habits is their educational component. An abundance of educational resources may be found on the internet, ranging from scholarly sections and e-books to online tutorials and courses. Thinking back on our digital learning practices requires evaluating how we use these tools to advance both personally and professionally. Do we use internet platforms to learn new things and expand our knowledge? Are we using online education to pursue lifetime learning? Do we engage in internet forums and communities to improve our educational experience? By using digital technologies for education, we may extend our horizons and discover new possibilities.

One aspect that is frequently disregarded is how our digital activities affect the environment. Electronic waste and environmental degradation are caused by the creation, use, and disposal of digital gadgets. Examining our digital behaviors with an eye on the environment means taking into account how sustainably we use our devices. Do we consider how long our digital devices will last? Do we recycle our old electronics or dispose of them properly? Do we back businesses that put an emphasis on sustainable practices? A more sustainable future can be achieved by adopting digital habits that are ecologically mindful.

Digital habits also affect our attention spans and cognitive capacities. Reduced focus and scattered attention might result from the constant onslaught of messages and information. Examining the ways in which digital gadgets impact our ability to focus and think clearly is part of reflecting on our cognitive digital habits. Are we utilizing digital devices and multitasking too much? Do we permit notifications to impede our productivity and cognitive processes? Are we regaining our attention and mental clarity by engaging in mindfulness and digital detoxification? By putting digital distraction management techniques into practice, we can improve our productivity and cognitive health.

Furthermore, we should pay attention to the ethical ramifications of our digital activities. The ethical use of artificial intelligence and data privacy are just two of the many ethical conundrums facing the digital age. Examining our ethical online behavior requires us to think about how our online behavior affects society as a whole. Do we endorse firms and ethical activities in the digital space? Do we understand how the technologies we use affect ethics? Are we supporting responsible technology usage and digital rights? A more just and equitable digital environment can be achieved by taking an ethical stance with our digital behaviors.

Finally, there a significant cultural and societal consequences of our digital behaviors. Digital platforms have a profound impact on cultural norms and societal values, impacting not only political movements but also fashion trends. Analyzing how our digital interactions impact societal and cultural dynamics is part of reflecting on our cultural digital habits. In our digital interactions, are we advocating for diversity and inclusivity? Do we realize how the stuff we share and consume affects culture? Are we promoting constructive social change through digital platforms? We may become more responsible digital citizens by being aware of how our digital habits affect society and culture.

In summary, assessing your present digital habits is a complex process that calls for an all-encompassing strategy. Examining the amount of time spent on digital activities, the effects on mental and physical health, the standard of social interactions, the harmony between creation and consumption, the administration of finances and digital footprints, the use of digital tools for education, the use of digital tools for the environment, the effects on cognition, the ethical implications, and the cultural and societal impact are all part of this process. We can develop better, more deliberate digital habits that improve our well-being and benefit the digital environment by thinking about these factors. In order to navigate the complexity of the digital world and make sure that our digital behaviors are consistent with our individual and societal values, this constant assessment is crucial.

Identifying digital clutter

Recognizing digital clutter is a skill that is becoming more and more important in our digitally advanced society. The increasing integration of digital devices and platforms into our daily lives can result in stress and inefficiency due to the buildup of extraneous data, files, and programs. Digital clutter can take many different forms, such as duplicate files on our PCs or an overwhelming amount of notifications on our smartphones, and it negatively affects both our mental and physical health. This section examines the idea of digital clutter, the ways it can appear, and practical methods for locating and handling it.

The buildup of superfluous or needless digital objects that make it difficult to use digital platforms and devices efficiently is known as "digital clutter." It consists of digital habits, emails, apps, files, and notifications that are no longer needed but take up significant time and space. Recognizing digital clutter and appreciating its effects is the first step in identifying it. Digital clutter can cause cognitive overload and lower productivity, much like physical clutter in our houses can wreak havoc and cause disorder. It is frequently characterized by feeling overwhelmed when sifting through files and programs, having trouble finding crucial information, and being constantly distracted by too many messages.

Files that are no longer needed or relevant are among the most prevalent types of digital clutter. Documents, pictures, films, and other information kept on our devices can be among them. We gather a tremendous amount of data over time, most of which is rendered outdated or irrelevant. In this case, identifying digital clutter is about routinely going through and sorting through our information. Organizing files into appropriate directories, getting rid of duplicates, and throwing away files that are unnecessary can all help achieve this. By giving essential documents a consolidated, easily accessible area and making it simple to remove extraneous stuff, cloud storage solutions can also aid in the management of file clutter.

Another important cause of digital disarray is email clutter. Every day, the typical person receives a lot of emails containing spam, commercial messages, and correspondence relating to their job. A packed inbox from a steady stream of emails might make it challenging to prioritize and reply to crucial correspondence. Identifying email clutter entails putting good email management techniques into practice. This entails removing yourself from pointless email lists, setting up filters to automatically sort new emails, and routinely archiving or deleting outdated correspondence. Establishing designated periods for email checks and responses can also help keep the inbox from getting out of control and lessen the psychological strain that comes with receiving emails all the time.

Our gadgets' software and applications can also add to digital clutter. App shops make it convenient to download a plethora of applications, many of which we use occasionally or entirely forget about. These unused programs might cause device performance to decrease in addition to taking up storage space. Finding application clutter entails periodically going over all of the installed programs to assess their value and relevancy. Apps that are no longer utilized or needed can be uninstalled to free up space on the device and increase its overall performance. Moreover, putting programs into folders according to their purpose or usage frequency can make the UI more efficient and user-friendly.

A common source of digital clutter is notifications from different platforms and apps, which can have a significant influence on our ability to concentrate and work efficiently. An uneven attention span and frequent disruptions can result from notifications that ping nonstop. Determining the need and frequency of these notifications is a necessary step in identifying notification clutter. Excessive notifications might be less disruptive by turning off non-essential notifications, personalizing notification settings for individual apps, and utilizing "Do Not Disturb" modes when working intently. Our ability to focus and work deeply can be enhanced by minimizing notification clutter.

Digital clutter includes all of our digital routines and actions in addition to actual files and programs. This encompasses the duration we dedicate to social media, the websites we often browse, and the electronic pursuits that capture our interest. Considering how we use our gadgets and the internet might help us recognize clutter in our digital habits. Are we wasting too much time on social media sites that don't improve our lives? Are we aimlessly perusing websites with no discernible purpose? Identifying and reducing digital clutter in our routines can be accomplished by participating in a digital detox, which involves purposefully limiting our use of particular digital activities. Establishing deliberate objectives for our usage of digital devices and monitoring our screen time can reveal areas that need improvement.

Another layer of digital clutter has been brought about by the growth of online services and digital subscriptions. The sheer number of digital subscriptions available might be daunting. They range from cloud storage and software licensing to streaming services and news subscriptions. Examining and assessing the subscriptions we now own is necessary to identify subscription clutter. Are we making use of every service for which we have a subscription? Exist any overlapping or superfluous subscriptions? Reducing unnecessary subscriptions and combining services can help us consume digital content more efficiently and spend less money.

Our digital imprint and online presence are also part of the digital clutter. This covers the digital footprints we leave behind, the data we share, and the accounts we create across several sites. Conducting an audit of our digital accounts and personal data is necessary to find clutter in our online presence. Do any of our accounts on websites or services exist anymore? Are we disclosing more private information on social media than is necessary? We may control and safeguard our digital footprint by deleting useless accounts, changing privacy settings, and exercising caution when sharing personal information online.

Digital clutter in the context of work settings can appear on platforms and collaboration technologies used for work. Tools, including communication platforms, shared files, and project management software, are frequently employed due to the increase in remote work and digital collaboration. Clutter and confusion, however, might result from the misuse or improper handling of these instruments. Clarifying rules for the use of collaboration technologies is essential to identifying digital clutter in work environments. This entails putting shared drives in order using consistent naming standards, archiving finished projects on a regular basis, and making sure that communication platforms are utilized efficiently to prevent information overload. Teams that adopt a digitally organized culture are more productive and experience less stress as a result of less digital clutter.

Digital clutter can also have an adverse effect on our wellbeing and mental health. Burnout, anxiety, and overwhelming emotions of information overload can result from the continual connectivity and flood of digital data. Recognizing the symptoms of digital weariness is essential to understanding the emotional and psychological effects of digital clutter. Do the demands of the digital age cause us to feel nervous or stressed all the time? Is it tough for us to step away from jobs or digital activities? The detrimental impacts of digital clutter on mental health can be lessened by putting digital well-being practices into practice, such as establishing boundaries for digital use, taking regular breaks from screens, and engaging in mindfulness exercises.

Another crucial factor to take into account is how digital clutter affects the environment. Electronic waste and environmental degradation are caused by the creation, usage, and disposal of digital gadgets. Assessing the sustainability of our device usage is a necessary step in determining the environmental impact of our digital habits. Are we replacing our electronics more often than is required? Are we discarding or recycling outdated devices in the right way? Reducing electronic waste and fostering a greener digital ecosystem can be achieved by endorsing sustainable practices and adopting environmentally responsible digital habits.

Digital clutter and financial management are related in the digital sphere. The convenience of digital transactions, online shopping, and subscription services can result in financial clutter and impulsive expenditure. Examining our digital spending patterns is necessary in order to identify financial clutter. Are we spending money online needlessly? Are we monitoring online purchases and subscriptions? Better financial health can be promoted, and digital financial clutter can be managed by putting budgeting tools into practice and routinely examining financial statements.

Moreover, the notion of digital minimalism provides a structure for recognizing and handling digital clutter. A more deliberate and conscientious attitude to digital consumption is promoted by digital minimalism. It entails clearing out digital spaces by concentrating on crucial digital tasks that complement our objectives and core beliefs. By carefully examining our digital lives, finding areas of excess, and purposefully cutting back on pointless digital activities, we can adopt digital minimalism. Adopting digital minimalism can help us establish a more meaningful and equitable relationship with technology.

Taking on digital clutter requires not just individual work but also more extensive organizational and societal activities. Promoting digital literacy and raising awareness of the effects of digital clutter are two aspects of this. Those who attend educational seminars and workshops on digital well-being, cybersecurity, and organization can become more adept at managing their digital life. By putting in place digital health initiatives, offering tools for digital detoxification, and encouraging a culture of conscientious digital use, organizations may also contribute.

To sum up, defining digital clutter is a complex process that entails identifying its different manifestations and comprehending how it affects our lives. Digital clutter can hinder work, have a negative impact on mental health, and degrade the environment. It can range from duplicate files and email overload to excessive notifications and digital addictions. We may establish a more productive and peaceful digital environment by implementing techniques to manage digital clutter, such as consistent file organization, efficient email management, careful usage of applications and notifications, and embracement of digital minimalism. Combining individual efforts with more extensive social measures to support digital literacy and well-being is necessary to address digital clutter. We may improve our quality of life and our relationship with technology by being proactive in identifying and eliminating digital clutter.

Recognizing the impact of technology on your life

Understanding how technology has affected your life requires a thorough analysis of the ways in which digital innovations have impacted our daily lives, relationships, jobs, and general well-being. It's critical to evaluate the complex effects of technology—both good and bad—on our personal and professional lives as it continues to advance at a rate never seen before. This section explores the various ways that technology influences our lives, including how it affects social dynamics, education, mental health, communication, productivity, and enjoyment.

The impact of technology on communication is among its most significant effects. The introduction of social media, instant messaging apps, and cell phones has completely changed the way people communicate with each other. With the use of these technologies, people may now communicate in real-time with friends, family, and coworkers anywhere in the world, despite geographical barriers. Social networks, phone messages, and video conversations provide constant connectedness, enabling us to keep in touch with each other no matter where we are in the world. But there are disadvantages to this constant connectedness as well. Reliance on digital communication can also result in shallow exchanges since text messages and emoticons frequently take the place of in-person discussions. This change may have an effect on the depth and caliber of our bonds, making us feel alone even when we are always in contact.

Productivity is one area where technology has a significant impact. Innovations in the workplace, like automation technologies, project management software, and cloud computing, have made labor more efficient and allowed for remote employment. Workers can now easily communicate with one another from anywhere in the globe, accessing shared documents and real-time updates. Traditional work environments have changed as a result of this flexibility, providing chances for the gig economy and independent workers as well as a better work-life balance. But the loss of distinction between work and personal life is the unintended consequence of this enhanced productivity. Being expected to be available at all times can cause stress and burnout in workers who find it difficult to put work aside outside of office hours.

Concern over how technology affects mental health is on the rise. Digital platforms offer online therapy, support groups, and mental health services, yet excessive screen time and social media consumption have been connected to a number of mental health problems. People who evaluate their lives against carefully selected highlights of others may have low self-esteem and feelings of inadequacy as a result of the comparison culture that social media promotes. Anxiety and shorter attention spans can also be caused by the constant barrage of information and notifications. In order to establish measures to offset the negative consequences, such as digital detoxes, mindfulness exercises, and setting boundaries for technology use, it is imperative to recognize these implications.

Technology has significantly changed the nature of education. Education obstacles have been removed through the democratization of knowledge access through online learning platforms, virtual classrooms, and educational apps. From the convenience of their homes, students may now access a multitude of resources, learn at their own speed, and take part in interactive learning activities. This has proven especially helpful during the COVID-19 outbreak, which caused disruptions to regular teaching environments. Nonetheless, because not every student has equal access to technology and the internet, the digital gap continues to be a severe problem. This discrepancy may make educational disparities worse, which would disadvantage confident kids. Additionally, some students may find it challenging to maintain their enthusiasm and self-discipline when switching to an online learning environment.

Technology has completely changed the entertainment sector by providing never-before-seen access to games, movies, music, and other media. Digital downloads, online gaming platforms, and streaming services offer us a wide variety of entertainment alternatives at our fingertips. Because of its accessibility, on-demand material has revolutionized the way we consume media, enabling us to watch or listen to whatever we want, whenever wc want. But as binge-watching and extended gaming sessions grow prevalent, this convenience may also contribute to overconsumption and inactive lifestyles. Maintaining a healthy balance between digital entertainment and social media, exercise, and other activities is crucial.

Technology has had a profound impact on social dynamics, changing how people establish and sustain connections. Social media platforms enable the creation of online communities and support networks by connecting users with like-minded individuals. Additionally, these platforms have been instrumental in social movements, bringing attention to and spurring action on a range of concerns. However, the internet's accessibility and anonymity may also breed bad habits like trolling, cyberbullying, and the dissemination of false information. Digital literacy and critical thinking abilities are necessary to navigate these social dynamics, identify reliable information, and promote constructive relationships online.

Our daily schedules and lifestyle preferences have also changed as a result of technology. Wearable technology, smartphone apps, and smart home appliances make managing our lives easier and more productive.

Technology has ingrained itself into our daily lives, from fitness monitors that keep an eye on our health to virtual assistants that aid with household chores. But our dependence on technology can also lead to dependency, which weakens our capacity for independent work. Technology must be used as a tool to improve our lives, not as a crutch that limits our potential.

Technology has significantly improved patient care, diagnosis, and treatment in the healthcare industry. Access to healthcare services and individualized treatment plans has been enhanced because of telemedicine, electronic health records, and wearable health monitors. Nowadays, patients can follow their health parameters in real time, receive immediate medical advice, and speak with doctors remotely. These developments could lead to better health and a higher standard of living. However, the use of technology in healthcare also brings up issues with data security and privacy. Using technology to improve healthcare must prioritize protecting and responsibly using patient information.

Technology has completely changed the financial management industry by providing a wide range of platforms and tools for investing, managing funds, and conducting transactions. When managing financial matters, robo-advisors, mobile payment apps, and online banking offer accessibility and convenience. These resources can save time, lower the possibility of mistakes, and assist people in making wise financial decisions. Online transactions' convenience, meanwhile, can also result in careless money management and reckless purchasing. In order to attain financial security and stability, it is critical to become digitally literate and use these tools appropriately.

Technology's effects on the environment are complicated issues that need to be carefully considered. On the one hand, technological advancements in energy-efficient appliances, smart grids, and renewable energy sources can help promote sustainability. On the other side, electronic waste and environmental deterioration are caused by the manufacturing and disposal of electronic gadgets. Understanding the impact of technology on the environment requires us to choose wisely when it comes to recycling, using our devices, and promoting sustainable habits. We can lessen technology's detrimental effects on the environment and work toward a more sustainable future by using it thoughtfully.

Technology provides people with previously unheard-of chances to express themselves creatively and artistically, allowing them to share their works with a worldwide audience. In order to interact with like-minded people and get credit for their work, artists, writers, singers, and creators can use social media platforms, blogs, and video-sharing websites. Our cultural environment has been enhanced by the various and inventive content produced as a result of the democratization of creativity. However, the urge to create and distribute material all the time can also result in burnout and creative fatigue. Striking a balance between using technology to express ourselves creatively and setting aside time to nurture and replenish our creative energies is crucial.

To sum up, understanding how technology affects your life entails a complex investigation of the ways in which technological innovations influence different facets of your life. In every aspect of our lives, technology is essential, from mental health and education to productivity and communication. While there are many advantages, including improved efficiency, connectedness, and information availability, there are drawbacks as well, like digital overload, privacy issues, and the possibility of detrimental effects on mental health. Through an awareness of these effects and the creation of technology management plans, we may maximize the positive aspects of technology while reducing its adverse effects. In order to successfully navigate the challenges of the digital age and make sure that technology is a vehicle for good growth and well-being, it is imperative that this constant evaluation be conducted.

Assessing the need for digital detox

Evaluating whether a digital detox is necessary requires a thorough analysis of our connection with technology and how much of it we use on a daily basis. Digital gadgets are now considered essential instruments for business, education, entertainment, and communication in the modern world. But our continual connectedness and reliance on technology may be seriously harming our mental, physical, and emotional health. The idea of a "digital detox," which comprises stepping away from electronics for a period of time in order to re-establish equilibrium and recalibrate, has drawn more attention in response to the problems associated with excessive technology use. This section explores the benefits of digital detoxification, the indicators that it's time for one, and practical tips for incorporating a digital detox into all facets of life. It also explores the reasons behind the growing demand for this kind of behavior.

The ubiquitous presence of digital devices has significantly transformed our lifestyle and interactions with the outside world. Gadgets such as laptops, tablets, and smartphones allow for accessible communication, immediate access to information, and a never-ending supply of entertainment. Undoubtedly, these developments have improved our lives in many ways, but they have also resulted in an over-dependence on technology, which frequently leads to digital overload. Combating the detrimental effects of this excess is one of the main reasons to think about going on a digital detox.

It can be challenging to focus on work and take part in meaningful activities when there is a constant barrage of notifications, emails, and social media updates. This can lead to feelings of urgency and anxiety. People can feel less stressed, focus better, and recover control over their time and attention by taking a break from digital devices.

The adverse effects of excessive screen time on physical health provide yet another strong argument for a digital detox. Extended usage of electronic devices has been linked to several health problems, such as headaches, disturbed sleep cycles, and eye strain. Screen blue light can disrupt melatonin production, a hormone that controls sleep, making it harder to fall asleep and remain asleep. Furthermore, a sedentary lifestyle linked to prolonged screen time can aggravate musculoskeletal issues, lead to bad posture, and raise the risk of chronic illnesses, including obesity and cardiovascular disease. A digital detox enables people to put down their devices, get moving, and create healthy routines that enhance their general wellbeing.

Another reason for the necessity of a digital detox is the effect that technology has on mental health. Digital gadgets give users access to helpful materials and social networks, but overuse of them can exacerbate depressive, anxious, and socially isolated symptoms. Social comparison is a phenomenon where people compare their own lives to the carefully chosen and frequently idealized representations of others. Social media platforms, in particular, have been connected to this phenomenon. This may result in low self-esteem, inadequate feelings, and a warped perception of reality. Additionally, people who experience digital fatigue—a state in which they feel emotionally and physically worn out—may be a result of the continual barrage of information and the need to stay connected. A digital detox provides a chance to detach from these pressures, reflect, and develop a positive relationship with technology.

In order to address the harmful consequences of technology use, it is imperative to recognize the signals that point to the need for a digital detox. The incapacity to switch off from digital devices is one of the primary indicators. It could be time to think about doing a detox if people find themselves continually checking their phones, experiencing anxiety when they are not online, or favoring digital relationships over in-person encounters. The effect on performance and productivity is another indicator. Overuse of screens can cause concentration problems, procrastination, and a reduction in work completion efficiency. A vacation from digital devices may also be indicated by behavioral and emotional changes, such as heightened irritation, restlessness, and disinterest in offline activities. People can take proactive measures to undertake a digital detox and regain balance in their lives by being aware of these indications.

Adopting a digital detox calls for careful preparation and a dedication to long-lasting adjustments. Establishing specific objectives and aspirations for the detox is one of the first tasks. This entails figuring out the precise elements of digital use that are stressing people out or impairing their wellbeing, as well as what the detox's intended results are. Whether your goal is to spend less time on screens, get better sleep, or strengthen your relationships, having a clear purpose can give you direction and drive. Establishing a supportive setting for the detox is another crucial component. This could entail discussing the detox with friends, family, and coworkers and asking for their cooperation and understanding. Creating limitations and boundaries on digital use—for example, designating specific hours or areas that are screen-free—can also aid in fostering an environment that is supportive of the detox.

Adding different activities to the daily schedule is a crucial tactic for a successful digital detox. A meaningful and pleasurable substitute for screen time can be found in physical activity, hobbies, time spent in nature, and social interactions. In addition to providing a diversion from the need to use electronics, these activities also foster social interactions, mental and physical well-being, and physical health. Furthermore, by encouraging a sense of peace and self-awareness, mindfulness and relaxation practices like journaling, deep breathing, and meditation might improve the detox experience. Through the incorporation of these activities into daily routines, people can establish a well-rounded and satisfying way of living that is not exclusively dependent on digital technology.

One more successful method for a digital detox is to cut back on screen time gradually as opposed to all at once. This entails establishing small objectives to cut back on digital use, such as restricting social media use to particular times of the day or cutting down on the amount of time spent in front of screens each week. Tracking and managing screen usage with apps and other digital well-being tools can yield insightful information and facilitate progress monitoring. It's also critical to be aware of the habits that people have when using digital media, such as checking social media or emails out of boredom or habit. People can choose to utilize technology in a more deliberate and meaningful way by being aware of these trends.

Reevaluating the use of digital tools and platforms may be part of implementing a digital detox in the context of work and productivity. This entails prioritizing tasks that don't require screen time, establishing boundaries for digital interactions linked to business, and optimizing routes of communication. Reducing digital tiredness and improving focus can be achieved by remote workers and those in digitally heavy jobs through regular breaks, Pomodoro Technique practice, and incorporating offline activities into the workday. Furthermore, companies can help staff members by supporting programs that promote digital well-being, offering tools for screen time management, and fostering a positive work-life balance.

A digital detox can improve the quality of time spent together and strengthen family bonds. Setting up times when the entire family is prohibited from using screens, including during meals or special family events, can promote in-person communication and shared experiences. Taking part in non-screen-related group activities like board games, hikes, or art projects can improve family ties and produce enduring memories. By controlling their own screen time and emphasizing the need to strike a balance between online and offline activities, parents can also serve as role models for healthy digital behaviors. A digital detox can improve the dynamics and well-being of the family by fostering a culture that values deep connections and experiences.

The principles of digital detoxification can also be beneficially implemented in educational contexts. By stressing to children the value of striking a balance between screen time and offline activities, educators and schools may help students become more digitally literate. This entails promoting physical activity, playing outside, and experiential learning. Introducing screen-free breaks throughout the school day and giving pupils the chance to participate in social and creative activities can promote their general growth and wellbeing. Teachers can also establish a learning atmosphere that promotes focus, engagement, and awareness by modeling good digital habits.

In summary, determining if a digital detox is necessary requires a careful analysis of the ways in which technology affects many facets of our lives. The benefits of a digital detox are numerous, ranging from the negative impact of excessive screen usage on relationships, productivity, and general well-being to the physical and mental health consequences. By identifying the warning signals of digital detoxification and putting effective techniques into practice, people can regain their equilibrium, lower their stress levels, and develop a more positive connection with technology. We can maximize technology's positive effects while reducing its negative ones by using it thoughtfully and intentionally, which will help us live more balanced and fulfilled lives in the digital era.

CHAPTER III

Decluttering Your Digital Space

Strategies for decluttering your digital devices

Decluttering digital devices has become increasingly important as our lives are intertwined with technology. The accumulation of unnecessary files, applications, and notifications can lead to inefficiency, distraction, and even stress. As digital devices become more integral to our personal and professional lives, maintaining an organized and efficient digital environment is crucial. This section explores comprehensive strategies for decluttering digital devices, delving into methods for organizing files, managing applications, optimizing device performance, and establishing sustainable digital habits.

The first step in decluttering digital devices involves understanding the scope of the clutter. Over time, we accumulate a significant amount of digital debris, ranging from outdated files and redundant applications to countless notifications and browser tabs. This clutter not only consumes storage space but also hinders productivity by making it difficult to locate important information and manage tasks efficiently. Recognizing the extent of digital clutter allows us to take proactive steps to address it.

One effective strategy for decluttering digital devices is organizing files and folders systematically. This process begins with conducting a thorough audit of all files stored on the device. Sorting files into categories based on their type and relevance can help identify duplicates and outdated items. For instance, documents, images, videos, and software can be grouped separately. Within these categories, further subcategorization by date, project, or subject matter can create a more intuitive structure. Deleting redundant files and archiving those that are rarely used but need to be retained can significantly free up storage space and improve accessibility.

Cloud storage solutions offer a practical way to manage files while reducing on-device clutter. Platforms like Google Drive, Dropbox, and OneDrive provide secure, easily accessible storage options that can be synchronized across multiple devices. By transferring less frequently accessed files to the cloud, users can maintain a cleaner local storage environment. Additionally, cloud storage offers the benefit of automatic backups, ensuring that important files are protected against device failures. Utilizing cloud storage also facilitates collaboration, as files can be shared and edited in real time by multiple users.

Email management is another critical aspect of digital decluttering. An overflowing inbox can be a significant source of stress and distraction. Implementing effective email management techniques can streamline communication and improve productivity. One approach is to adopt the "Inbox Zero" method, which involves processing each email as it arrives and categorizing it into actionable, reference, or disposable items. Actionable emails require a response or follow-up, reference emails are stored for future use, and disposable emails are deleted or archived. Setting up filters and rules to automatically sort incoming emails can further enhance this process by directing messages to designated folders based on sender or subject.

Unsubscribing from unnecessary mailing lists and newsletters can also reduce email clutter. Many of us subscribe to various services that we no longer find helpful or relevant. Periodically reviewing and unsubscribing from these lists can decrease the volume of incoming emails and make it easier to focus on essential communications. Additionally, setting aside specific times each day to check and respond to emails, rather than continuously monitoring the inbox, can help manage time more effectively and reduce interruptions.

Application management is another vital component of digital decluttering. Over time, we tend to accumulate numerous applications, many of which are rarely used or entirely forgotten. These unused apps not only take up valuable storage space but can also impact device performance. Conducting a periodic review of installed applications and evaluating their necessity can help identify those that can be uninstalled. For essential applications that are used frequently, ensuring they are updated to the latest versions can enhance security and functionality.

Organizing applications into folders based on their function or frequency of use can create a more streamlined and user-friendly interface. For example, productivity apps can be grouped together, while entertainment apps can be placed in a separate folder. This categorization makes it easier to locate and access applications when needed, reducing the time spent searching for specific tools.

Managing notifications is essential for maintaining focus and minimizing distractions. Digital devices generate a constant stream of notifications from various applications, including emails, social media, messaging apps, and news alerts. These notifications can interrupt workflow and lead to a fragmented attention span. One strategy to manage notifications effectively is to customize settings for each application, allowing only essential notifications to come through. For instance, work-related apps can be set to deliver notifications immediately, while social media alerts can be muted or limited to specific times of the day. Utilizing "Do Not Disturb" modes during periods of focused work can further reduce interruptions and enhance productivity.

Browser management is another aspect of digital decluttering that can significantly impact efficiency. Many users tend to keep multiple browser tabs open simultaneously, leading to cluttered and disorganized browsing sessions. Organizing browser bookmarks into folders based on topics or frequently visited sites can help streamline web navigation. Additionally, regularly reviewing and closing unused tabs can prevent browser slowdown and make it easier to focus on the task at hand. Utilizing browser extensions that assist in managing tabs and bookmarks can also be beneficial in maintaining an organized browsing environment.

Optimizing device performance is a crucial part of digital decluttering. Over time, digital devices can become sluggish due to the accumulation of temporary files, cache data, and background processes. Performing regular maintenance tasks such as clearing the cache, deleting temporary files, and uninstalling unused programs can enhance device performance and free up valuable resources. Many operating systems offer built-in tools for disk cleanup and system optimization, making it easy to perform these tasks periodically.

Security is another crucial consideration when decluttering digital devices. Ensuring that all software and applications are up to date with the latest security patches can protect against vulnerabilities and potential threats. Utilizing antivirus and anti-malware tools can provide an additional layer of protection, safeguarding personal and sensitive information. Regularly backing up important data to external drives or cloud storage can prevent data loss in case of device failure or cyberattacks.

Establishing sustainable digital habits is essential for maintaining a clutter-free digital environment over the long term. This involves developing routines and practices that promote organization and efficiency. For instance, setting aside time each week to review and organize files, emails, and applications can prevent clutter from accumulating. Practicing mindful digital consumption, such as being selective about the apps installed and the notifications enabled, can help maintain focus and reduce distractions. Additionally, periodically evaluating and adjusting digital habits to align with personal and professional goals can ensure that technology use remains purposeful and beneficial.

Digital minimalism is a philosophy that can guide efforts to declutter digital devices. This approach advocates for a more intentional and mindful use of technology, focusing on tools and activities that add value and enhance well-being. Adopting digital minimalism involves critically assessing the necessity and impact of each digital tool and eliminating those that do not contribute positively to one's life. By prioritizing meaningful digital interactions and minimizing digital distractions, individuals can create a more balanced and fulfilling relationship with technology.

In the professional realm, digital decluttering can enhance productivity and efficiency. Organizing digital workspaces, such as virtual desktops and project management platforms, can streamline workflows and improve collaboration. Establishing clear naming conventions and folder structures for shared drives can facilitate more accessible access to essential documents and reduce time spent searching for files. Additionally, setting boundaries for digital communication, such as designated email response times and meeting-free periods, can help manage workload and prevent burnout.

For students and educators, digital decluttering can support a more effective learning environment. Organizing digital study materials, lecture notes, and assignments into categorized folders can improve accessibility and reduce stress. Utilizing educational platforms and tools that offer streamlined interfaces and integration with other resources can enhance the learning experience. Encouraging students to practice digital hygiene, such as regularly reviewing and deleting unnecessary files, can instill habits that promote long-term digital organization.

Families can also benefit from digital decluttering by creating a more harmonious home environment. Establishing screen-free zones or times, such as during meals or family activities, can encourage face-to-face interactions and strengthen relationships. Organizing shared digital resources, such as family photos and videos, into easily accessible and well-labeled folders can preserve memories and reduce digital chaos. Teaching children about the importance of digital organization and responsible technology use can help them develop healthy digital habits from a young age.

In conclusion, decluttering digital devices involves a multifaceted approach that encompasses organizing files, managing applications, optimizing device performance, and establishing sustainable digital habits. By systematically addressing each aspect of digital clutter, individuals can create a more efficient, productive, and stress-free digital environment. The benefits of digital decluttering extend beyond improved device performance; they also enhance mental clarity, reduce stress, and promote a healthier relationship with technology. As digital devices continue to play a central role in our lives, adopting strategies for digital decluttering is essential for maintaining balance and well-being in the digital age. By prioritizing intentional and mindful use of technology, we can harness its benefits while mitigating its drawbacks, leading to a more fulfilling and organized digital experience.

Organizing digital files and data

In today's technology-driven society, when enormous amounts of information are saved and managed electronically, organizing digital files and data is a crucial activity. This section addresses the need to keep digital files and data organized, examines several approaches and methods for achieving effective organization, and talks about the advantages of maintaining a structured digital environment. Through the implementation of efficient file management techniques, both individuals and companies can improve productivity, guarantee data security, and cultivate a digital workspace that is more efficient and easily accessible.

It is impossible to exaggerate the significance of digital files and data organization. The amount of digital data that is created, shared, and preserved in this day and age can quickly become overwhelming. When organizing without a methodical strategy, significant time and resources are lost looking for files, which lowers productivity and increases irritation. Moreover, dispersed and poorly maintained digital assets increase the chance of data loss or security breaches. An efficient digital workspace reduces stress levels, encourages productivity, and offers a solid platform for efficient data management and retrieval.

The creation of an understandable and rational folder structure is an essential component of digital files and data organization. Finding and accessing files can be made much easier by organizing folders and subfolders into a hierarchical structure based on projects, categories, or themes. For example, grouping files according to the project name, month, or year might offer a contextual or chronological structure that makes navigating easier. Subfolders can be created inside each main folder to better organize data and make sure relevant papers are kept together. In addition to facilitating better file retrieval, this hierarchical structure reduces the possibility of losing or misplacing crucial data.

Maintaining an orderly digital environment requires using descriptive and consistent naming standards for files and folders. Using a uniform naming convention guarantees that files can be found and identified with ease. Clarity and context can be added by including pertinent information in the filenames, such as dates, project names, and file versions. Consider using names like "2023_Project_Report_V1" or "ClientProposal_June2023" in place of more general ones like "Document1" or "File_A," as they can quickly convey important information. Maintaining uniformity in naming conventions also helps to avoid misunderstanding and duplication, which, over time, facilitates file management and location.

Data about data, or metadata, is essential for improving searchability and structuring digital files. Information like file type, author, creation date, keywords, and tags are examples of metadata. More sophisticated and effective search features are made possible by using metadata, allowing users to easily filter and find specific files based on a variety of factors. Users can add, change, and search information for individual files using built-in metadata management tools found in many operating systems and software programs. Both individuals and businesses can build a digital repository that is easier to search and more structured by utilizing metadata.

The organization and accessibility of digital assets have been completely transformed by cloud storage options. Storage alternatives that are safe, scalable, and quickly available and that can be synchronized across numerous devices are offered by platforms like Google Drive, Dropbox, and Microsoft OneDrive. In addition to minimizing the need for physical storage devices, cloud storage provides sophisticated file management functionalities, including sharing, version control, and collaboration. Users may consolidate their file storage, guarantee data redundancy with automatic backups, and enable smooth team collaboration by employing cloud storage. Furthermore, flexibility and convenience are improved by having file access from any location with an internet connection.

Over time, keeping an orderly digital environment requires putting in place a regular file management regimen. Digital files and data benefit from routine inspection and cleansing, just like physical environments need to be cleaned and organized on a regular basis. Digital clutter can be avoided by scheduling a specific time to browse through files, remove duplicates or unneeded objects, and archive outdated or rarely viewed files. Transferring files to an archive folder or location that are no longer in use but must be kept for compliance or reference is known as archiving. This procedure keeps the active working area organized and productive, in addition to freeing up storage space.

A crucial component of maintaining digital data, particularly in collaborative or project-based environments, is version control. Without a methodical approach, managing several versions of a document or file can be difficult. Putting version control procedures into practice entails keeping an accurate log of all the modifications, additions, and deletions done to a file over time. This can be accomplished by using version control facilities offered by software programs and naming standards that contain dates or version numbers. Version control provides a historical record of modifications, enabling users to go back to earlier versions if necessary, in addition to preventing confusion and disputes resulting from various versions.

Having backup and disaster recovery plans is essential to managing digital files and data. Regular file backups guard against data loss brought on by hardware malfunctions, hacker assaults, or inadvertent deletion. Backup options include network-attached storage (NAS) systems, external hard drives, and automated cloud backups. Setting up a backup schedule and ensuring that backups are done correctly and consistently are crucial. Having a disaster recovery plan in place, in addition to routine backups, clarifies what should be done in the case of data loss or system failure, minimizing downtime and guaranteeing that critical files can be restored quickly.

Managing emails well is an essential part of digital data organization, especially in work environments where email correspondence is everyday. A cluttered inbox can hinder work and make it challenging to find crucial messages. Order can be maintained by putting email management strategies into practice, such as the "Inbox Zero" strategy, which aims to keep the inbox empty or almost empty. Processing each email as it comes in, classifying it as disposable, reference, or actionable, and then transferring it to the relevant folder are all part of this procedure. Emails can be further organized and retrieval streamlined by creating folders and subfolders within the email client based on projects, clients, or themes. Incoming emails can also be automatically sorted by rules and filters, which minimizes manual labor and guarantees that messages are sent to the appropriate folders.

Owing to the amount and diversity of content, organizing digital images and media files poses particular difficulties. Organizing images in a methodical manner entails making folders according to occasions, seasons, or subjects. By using metadata and tags, media files can be made more searchable, making it easier for users to find particular images or movies. Features like face recognition, geotagging, and automated categorization are available in many photo management software programs, which helps streamline the organizing process. Maintaining an orderly and clutter-free media library can also be achieved by routinely going through and getting rid of duplicate or low-quality pictures.

Organizations can streamline digital file organization and retrieval by putting in place a document management system (DMS). Document and record management, tracking, and archiving are all made possible by a DMS, which offers a central repository. Security and accessibility are improved by features like version control, access rights, and document indexing. Collaboration is further enhanced with a DMS, which enables numerous users to collaborate on documents at once and monitor changes instantly. Organizations can lower the risk of data loss or mismanagement, maintain regulatory compliance, and increase workflow efficiency by implementing a DMS.

Long-term success requires not only technical tactics but also cultivating a digital organizational culture within a team or company. A group's commitment to digital organization can be strengthened by promoting best practices for file management, such as consistent naming conventions, routine maintenance, and adherence to version control systems. Educating staff members on efficient digital file management methods can help improve their knowledge and abilities. Digital chaos is less likely when teams prioritize digital organization as a fundamental component of the corporate culture. This allows teams to operate more productively and cooperatively.

Since mobile devices are being utilized more and more for both personal and business purposes, it is essential to handle digital files and data effectively on these devices as well. On mobile devices, folders should be created, and apps should be categorized according to their usage or function. Device speed can be enhanced, and storage space can be freed up by routinely checking and removing unnecessary apps. By making use of cloud storage and synchronization services, one may lessen the dependence on local storage and guarantee that crucial information is accessible across devices. Smart passwords, biometric authentication, and remote wipe features are a few examples of security measures that may be put in place to safeguard private information on mobile devices and stop unwanted access.

Another crucial component of organizing digital data is managing browsers. Many people have a tendency to open many tabs at once, which makes for a cluttered and chaotic browsing experience. Putting bookmarks in folders according to subjects or websites you visit often can help you navigate the web more quickly and efficiently. Clearing out and discarding bookmarks on a regular basis helps keep clutter from building up. Using browser extensions to help you manage bookmarks and tabs will improve the efficiency and organization of your browsing even further. Furthermore, browser security and efficiency can be enhanced by routinely deleting cookies and cache.

Effective management of digital tools and software applications is another aspect of digital organization. Numerous people and institutions depend on an extensive array of software programs for diverse purposes, encompassing project administration, correspondence, and design, as well as data examination. Ensuring that tools are utilized effectively and securely requires regular monitoring of software licenses, upgrades, and configurations. Effective management of software assets can be achieved by putting in place a software inventory system that keeps track of information like update schedules, license keys, and installation dates. Software programs should be reviewed and updated on a regular basis to guarantee that they acquire the most recent security updates and are still compatible with other systems.

Online accounts and social media platforms can also benefit from the application of digital organization concepts. Maintaining social media profiles entails routinely checking and adjusting connections, privacy settings, and account settings. Putting followers and contacts into lists or groups helps improve interaction and communication. Managing several accounts can be made more accessible by using social media management solutions that provide functions like content curation, analytics, and scheduled updates. Furthermore, you can improve security and lessen digital clutter by routinely checking and eliminating accounts that are unnecessary or inactive.

Managing digital subscriptions and services is a subset of organizing digital files and data. Numerous people and institutions have subscriptions to a range of internet services, including online periodicals, software-as-a-service (SaaS) apps, and streaming platforms. Monitoring subscription specifics, billing cycles, and usage trends helps control costs and guarantee that subscriptions are utilized efficiently. Digital subscriptions can be managed more effectively by putting in place a subscription management system that keeps track of subscriber information and issues reminders for cancellations or renewals.

In summary, digital file and data organization is a complex process that includes creating logical and unambiguous folder structures, naming conventions that are consistent, utilizing cloud storage, leveraging metadata, putting regular maintenance schedules in place, and cultivating a culture of digital organization. Through the implementation of these tactics, both individuals and institutions can establish a digital environment that is secure, productive, and efficient. Beyond easier file retrieval and less clutter, digital organizing also boosts productivity, protects data, and creates a more accessible and efficient digital workspace. Effective digital organization will become even more crucial as the amount of digital data grows, making it a necessary talent for navigating the digital age. Individuals and organizations can fully utilize digital resources to increase productivity, collaboration, and success in both personal and professional efforts by setting priorities and putting good digital file management practices into practice.

Managing digital subscriptions and accounts

In the present world, when digital services are ingrained in every part of our lives, being able to manage digital subscriptions and accounts has become vital. Subscriptions are essential in both the personal and professional realms, from online publications to cloud storage options, from streaming platforms to software-as-a-service (SaaS) applications. These services are convenient and beneficial, but they also present issues when it comes to cost control, security, and preventing service overlaps. In-depth discussion of techniques, resources, and best practices for handling digital accounts and subscriptions is provided in this section. Topics include tracking subscriptions, maximizing usage, maintaining security, controlling expenses, and creating long-lasting digital habits.

In the digital age, effectively managing subscriptions starts with having a deep awareness of the services that one is subscribed to. A vast array of services are covered by digital subscriptions, such as news and magazine subscriptions, online learning platforms, cloud storage services, productivity tools like Microsoft Office 365 and Adobe Creative Cloud, and entertainment platforms like Netflix and Spotify. Even though each membership has its own set of advantages, there are charges involved that can mount up quickly. As a result, the first step in managing digital subscriptions is to inventory all of the services that are subscribed to and thoroughly and systematically catalog them.

It is imperative to compile a comprehensive list of all digital subscriptions. The name of the service, the kind of membership (monthly, annual, etc.), the price, the billing cycle, and any perks or usage restrictions should all be included in this entry. This record can be kept up to date with the use of tools like spreadsheets, specialized subscription management apps, or even built-in capabilities in some personal finance software. This list is kept up to date regularly to reflect the addition of new subscriptions and cancellations of existing ones, ensuring that it is a trustworthy resource for efficiently managing digital subscriptions.

The following stage is to evaluate the need and usage of each subscription after a thorough list has been created. Many people and businesses make the mistake of subscribing to several services that fulfill comparable functions, which results in duplication of effort and resource waste. Finding out which services are underutilized or redundant and which are actively used can be accomplished by conducting a utilization audit. For example, it could be a good idea to cancel the other streaming services if you subscribe to numerous of them but only use one of them frequently. Similar to this, if you have many productivity tools, you can streamline subscriptions and cut costs by comparing their distinct features and figuring out if one application can meet all of your demands.

Managing expenses is essential when it comes to digital subscriptions. Recurring expenses associated with subscriptions can result in unanticipated financial pressures if they are not watched. It's sensible to budget for digital subscriptions in order to control spending. This entails setting aside a set amount of money for subscriptions every month or every year and making sure the entire cost stays within this budget. Finding any differences and making the required corrections is made more accessible by routinely analyzing subscription expenses and comparing them to the budget that has been set aside.

Numerous online sites have tiers of subscription plans with different prices and levels of access. Assessing the attributes and advantages of every tier can aid in ascertaining the most economical scheme. For instance, a lower-tier plan might be enough, while a higher-tier plan offers extra services that are not necessary. On the other hand, certain providers' bundling of services might result in cost savings. For example, it may be less expensive to subscribe to a bundle that contains a music service and a streaming service than to subscribe to each separately.

Another smart way to manage digital subscriptions is to create reminders for subscription renewals and automate payments. Numerous services provide options for automatic renewal, which can help avoid service interruptions but, if left unchecked, can potentially result in accidental renewals. It is possible to assess whether the subscription is still necessary and if it fits within the budget by setting reminders a few days before the renewal date. This proactive strategy avoids unintentional charges and gives users the option to change or cancel subscriptions as needed.

When it comes to managing digital subscriptions and accounts, security is the top priority. Personal and financial information is frequently needed for each subscription; this data must be secured against unwanted access. The first line of defense: provide each account with a robust and one-of-a-kind password. In order to create and maintain complicated passwords that are both safe and easy to remember, password managers can be of assistance. By demanding a second form of verification in addition to the password, two-factor authentication (2FA) offers an extra layer of security. This can considerably lower the possibility of unwanted access even in the event that the password is stolen.

Sustaining security requires keeping an eye out for unusual activities across all subscriber accounts. Finding any illegal charges or strange login attempts can be aided by routinely reviewing activity logs and account statements. It is recommended to enable alerts for suspicious activity from various providers in order to receive timely notifications. Knowing how to promptly update payment details, change passwords, and get in touch with the service provider will help minimize potential harm in the event of a security breach.

Families and groups frequently share subscriptions, particularly for services that let several people utilize a single account. Subscription sharing can be economical, but it also needs to be carefully managed to guarantee security and equitable use. Misuse can be avoided by defining explicit rules about who is allowed access to shared subscriptions and by routinely checking user access. Furthermore, it's critical to comprehend the terms of service pertaining to account sharing because certain services may impose limitations or charge fees for sharing more than a specific amount.

Apps and tools for managing subscriptions have become essential tools for managing digital subscriptions. These programs have features like usage analytics, renewal reminders, cost tracking for subscriptions, and even assistance with finding and canceling unneeded subscriptions. Popular subscription management solutions with a variety of features catered to specific needs are Truebill, Subby, and Bobby. These programs offer a consolidated dashboard for managing subscriptions and can instantly detect them by integrating them with email inboxes and bank accounts.

Managing digital subscriptions in a business setting can be much more complicated because it involves numerous users, departments, and financial accounts. Simplifying the process and guaranteeing accountability can be achieved by implementing a centralized subscription management system within a company. This system can handle licenses and access permissions, track all subscriptions utilized within the company, and combine billing. It is possible to find unused subscriptions and save expenses by conducting routine audits of software and service usage. It is ensured that new subscriptions are in line with organizational needs and financial restrictions by establishing a straightforward process for subscription requests and approvals.

Additional factors to take into account while handling digital subscriptions in a professional setting include data protection and compliance. Protecting sensitive data requires ensuring that subscribing services abide by applicable data protection laws, such as the CCPA or GDPR. To reduce risks, go over each service's privacy policies and data handling procedures. Enhancing compliance and data protection initiatives might also involve keeping records of data processing agreements and doing routine security evaluations of subscribing services.

Managing digital subscriptions has both potential and challenges with the development of free trials and introductory offers. Before committing to a paid subscription, consumers can test out the features and advantages of a service via free trials. They do, however, also need to be managed carefully to prevent automated charges after the trial time expires. Unwanted costs can be avoided by setting reminders for trial expiration dates and deciding whether to continue or stop the subscription before the trial finishes. Making an informed decision on whether to continue with a paid subscription is aided by assessing the worth and usefulness of the service during the trial time.

In both personal and professional settings, communication and collaboration tools have grown essential, with subscriptions to services like Zoom, Slack, and Microsoft Teams becoming the norm. In addition to monitoring expenses, managing these subscriptions entails maximizing usage. Paying too much for features that aren't used can be avoided by making sure the right plans are chosen depending on the number of users and necessary features. Furthermore, productivity can be increased, and the return on investment can be maximized by training users on how to use these technologies effectively.

Entertainment streaming services, including music and video platforms, are some of the most widely used digital subscriptions. Keeping track of these subscriptions requires striking a balance between the range of content available, individual tastes, and financial limitations. Analyzing listening and watching habits on a regular basis might assist in identifying the services that offer the best value. For example, it may be worthwhile to cancel a streaming service that isn't utilized much in favor of one that is used more often. In addition, a lot of streaming services include family or group plans, which are sometimes more affordable for larger households.

The popularity of online learning platforms has increased since they provide tutorials, courses, and instructional materials for subscribers. Aligning subscriptions to these platforms with professional development and learning objectives is part of managing them. Evaluating course progress and completion rates on a regular basis might assist in determining the subscription value. It may be helpful to terminate the subscription or move to a better platform if any courses or content are no longer relevant. Access to educational resources can be improved, and costs can be decreased by utilizing employer-sponsored learning programs, discounts, and scholarships.

Cloud storage services, which offer subscriptions for different storage sizes and features, are crucial for managing data on a personal and professional level. Keeping track of these subscriptions entails determining storage requirements and making sure the chosen plan offers enough functionality and space. Optimizing storage use and maybe cutting expenses can be achieved by routinely going over saved data and removing pointless files. Additionally, data integrity and accessibility are improved by making sure that data is safeguarded and backed up using secure cloud storage options.

A syndrome known as "subscription fatigue" occurs when the abundance of subscription services causes overwhelm and financial stress. Effectively managing digital subscriptions entails identifying the symptoms of subscription weariness and addressing them. This may entail limiting the number of subscriptions kept active, prioritizing necessary services, and combining subscriptions. It is possible to avoid subscription fatigue and make sure that resources are going to the most valuable services by routinely going through and organizing subscriptions.

Long-term administration of digital accounts and subscriptions requires the development of sustainable digital habits. This entails fostering an understanding of the advantages and costs of subscriptions, routinely assessing and optimizing consumption, and upholding security and privacy. Sustainable digital habits include being proactive in handling renewals and cancellations, keeping up with changes in features or pricing, and educating oneself about the terms and conditions of each service. Furthermore, encouraging a deliberate approach to joining new services by assessing their worth and requirements helps avoid rash or unnecessary memberships.

To sum up, overseeing digital accounts and subscriptions is a complex undertaking that calls for a planned and proactive strategy. Digital subscriptions can be managed by individuals and organizations through the use of subscription management tools, cost management, security, and the creation of a centralized record of all subscriptions, as well as by tracking expenses and consumption. Effective subscription management improves productivity, security, and digital well-being in addition to financial savings. The ever-changing digital ecosystem necessitates the development of sustainable digital habits and ongoing education about best practices in order to navigate the multitude of subscription services accessible. Digital subscriptions can be fully utilized to provide convenience, value, and enrichment in both personal and professional spheres with careful and knowledgeable administration.

Implementing minimalist design principles in digital spaces

A strategy that prioritizes simplicity, clarity, and focus is the application of minimalist design concepts in digital settings. In digital design, minimalism aims to eliminate extraneous details and clutter so that the main idea or functionality is seen. This design concept has its roots in the more significant minimalist movement, which promotes focusing on what's essential and minimizing distractions. This translates into the creation of simple, clear, and functional interfaces in digital design. This paper investigates the fundamentals of minimalist design, how it's used in diverse digital settings, and the advantages and drawbacks of this methodology.

Its simplicity is what defines minimalist design. The maxim "less is more" sums up the notion that a more efficient and pleasurable user experience might result from having fewer things on a screen. Functionality and utility are prioritized over ostentatious embellishments and ornamentation in minimalist design. This method entails giving each design element considerable thought to make sure it serves the interface's overall goal. Every element in a minimalist design needs to justify its position by improving the user experience or fulfilling a distinct purpose.

A key component of minimalist design is whitespace, sometimes known as negative space. It describes the voids that exist on a screen between and around items. By reducing clutter, whitespace makes interfaces simpler to use and comprehend. It allows space between pieces so that users can concentrate on the most crucial areas of the interface. Making good use of whitespace can improve readability, highlight important details, and establish harmony and balance. It also helps to create the minimalist aesthetic's signature of simplicity and unclutteredness.

An essential component of minimalist design is typography. The general appearance and atmosphere of a digital area can be significantly influenced by the typefaces chosen, their sizes, and their application. Simple, sans-serif fonts that are easy to read and do not detract from the content are frequently preferred in minimalist design. A digital environment that uses consistent font looks more put together and professional. Users can be guided through the material in an understandable and logical way by using varying font sizes and weights in a hierarchical manner to highlight headers, subheadings, and body text.

Another essential component of minimalist design is color. A minimalist color scheme usually consists of a small number of hues, frequently emphasizing neutral shades such as grey, black, and white. The information can take center stage because of the sleek and elegant appearance that these colors generate. When using accent colors, utilize them sparingly to highlight critical components like buttons or calls to action. While preserving a feeling of simplicity and coherence, a digital space can benefit from the thoughtful selection and application of color.

In minimalist design, imagery is used with thoughtfulness and restraint. Minimalist design prioritizes a small number of excellent images that complement the text and improve the user experience over a large number of images throughout the digital environment. Pictures should be valuable and relevant; they should not only be decorative. Instead, they should add value. Large, striking graphics that make a powerful visual statement without overpowering the user are frequently used in minimalist design. The same idea applies to the usage of icons, which include straightforward, instantly identifiable symbols that facilitate understanding and navigation.

In minimalist design, navigation is essential. A well-designed navigation system should be simple to use and intuitive so that users can locate what they're looking for quickly. This frequently entails making menus more straightforward and limiting the amount of options available at any one moment. For instance, hamburger menus are a common element in minimalist design because they simplify the main interface by concealing less-used items behind a single icon. A smoother and more pleasurable user experience is facilitated by consistent and straightforward navigation, which also helps users feel more in control and lowers cognitive strain.

In contemporary digital design, responsiveness is crucial, and interfaces that function well across a variety of screens and devices can be created using minimalist design principles. The ease of adapting layouts to different settings is facilitated by the simplicity and clarity of minimalist design, which guarantees a consistent user experience across desktop, tablet, and smartphone platforms. Using responsive design strategies, such as scaled graphics and flexible grids, is essential to adopting minimalist design in a way that keeps its integrity both aesthetically and functionally across all devices.

Beyond its aesthetic appeal, minimalist design offers valuable advantages that can improve the functionality and usability of digital environments. For instance, since there are fewer items to load and render, simpler designs frequently have faster load times. This can enhance the user experience in general, especially for those with less powerful devices or slower internet connections. Furthermore, because there are fewer moving parts and components to maintain and troubleshoot, minimalist design can facilitate upgrades and maintenance. Long-term, this can result in lower costs and more efficiency.

The core of minimalist design is the user experience (UX). Users can have a more intuitive and pleasurable experience with minimalist design by concentrating on the essential components and eliminating distractions. This entails comprehending human demands and behaviors and creating interfaces that minimize obstacles to users' goals. In order to get insight into how users interact with the interface and identify areas for development, user testing, and feedback are essential components of this process. Effective minimalist design implementation requires the use of iterative design, which uses user feedback to improve and fine-tune the interface.

An essential factor in minimalist design is accessibility. Ensuring accessibility for those with impairments in digital spaces is not only a matter of law in numerous jurisdictions but also a matter of ethics. Clean, uncomplicated interfaces that are simpler to use with assistive technology are one way that minimalist design can promote accessibility. For persons with visual impairments, for instance, using a strong contrast between the text and background can increase readability. Users with cognitive disabilities can benefit from consistent, straightforward navigation as well as labeling for buttons and links that are descriptive. To further improve accessibility, make sure that any interactive features can be accessed using a keyboard and that any audiovisual content comes with transcripts or alternate text.

There are several essential phases involved in putting minimalist design concepts into practice. Identifying the objectives and purpose of the digital environment is the first stage. Prioritizing the most crucial components and guiding design decisions will come from knowing the goals of the digital space and the intended audience. This entails figuring out what essential functionality and content are and separating them from auxiliary or decorative components that might be reduced or eliminated.

The digital realm should then be prototyped or wireframed by designers. It is possible to experiment with layout and organization without becoming mired down in minutiae because of this low-fidelity representation. Wireframes serve as a template for the final design, concentrating on element placement and user experience flow. This phase is essential for determining how the minimalism principles will be implemented and for making changes prior to the start of more intricate design work.

The visual design can be created by designers once the wireframe is complete. This entails choosing minimalist-friendly fonts, colors, images, and other visual components. It's critical to keep assessing how each element contributes to the overall design during this process and to eliminate anything that doesn't have a clear function. The objective is to design a unified, aesthetically pleasing interface that improves user experience while removing superfluous distractions.

A crucial step in putting minimalist design into practice is user testing. Accurate user testing of the design yields insightful input on how well the interface satisfies their demands and identifies areas for improvement. The ultimate design is made more functional and aesthetically pleasing through this iterative testing and improvement process. In order to make sure that the design is inclusive and useable by everyone, it also assists in identifying any accessibility concerns that require attention.

The phase of implementation commences upon the completion of the design. Whether it is a website, application, or other digital product, this entails coding the design into a functional digital area. When it comes to bringing the design to life, developers are essential because they make sure that the end result upholds minimalism's tenets while still providing functionality and performance. At this stage, cooperation between developers and designers is crucial to resolving any technical issues and guaranteeing that the design is implemented.

It's critical to keep an eye on and maintain the digital space after launch. This entails routinely analyzing performance measurements, user feedback, and any modifications to technology or human behavior that may have an effect on the design. Maintaining the digital space's relevance and effectiveness through constant updates and enhancements ensures that users will continue to have a great experience.

Many digital places, such as websites, mobile applications, software interfaces, and even digital marketing materials, can benefit from the use of minimalist design. The design process is guided by the ideals of simplicity, clarity, and focus in every setting. Minimalist website design can improve readability and navigability by giving a website a polished, uncluttered look. It can result in user-friendly interfaces for mobile apps that are simple to use on tiny screens. It can simplify processes and lessen cognitive strain on software interfaces, improving tool efficiency and usability. It may produce visually striking and powerful content for digital marketing materials that effectively grab readers' attention and convey messages.

There are several advantages to minimalist design. The user experience can be improved and usefulness increased with minimalist design by eliminating unnecessary elements and concentrating on what matters most. Improved performance, quicker load times, and more straightforward maintenance are possible outcomes. Additionally, it might provide the image of being more polished and unified, strengthening user confidence and brand identity. Additionally, accessibility can be supported by minimalist design, increasing the inclusivity and usability of digital places for individuals with disabilities.

However, there are drawbacks to putting the minimalist design into practice. Finding the ideal ratio of utility to simplicity is one of the biggest obstacles. Eliminating extraneous components is vital, but it's also critical to make sure the interface works and meets user needs. To determine the ideal equilibrium, much thought and testing are needed. Fighting the need to gradually add more features or ornamentation is another difficulty. Sustaining a minimalist design calls for constant self-control and dedication to the ideas of focus and simplicity.

In addition, not every situation will lend itself to minimalist design. Users may occasionally favor interfaces with more excellent features and visual appeal, especially in environments where aesthetics and user engagement are essential, like gaming or entertainment platforms. Determining whether minimalist design is the best strategy requires an understanding of the target audience's tastes and behaviors.

In summary, applying the concepts of minimalist design to digital spaces necessitates a methodical and intentional approach to designing user interfaces that are efficient, intuitive, and aesthetically pleasing. Minimalist design can help accessibility, performance, and usability by emphasizing simplicity, clarity, and concentration. The creation of interfaces that concentrate vital content and functionality while minimizing distractions is guided by the principles of minimalist design, which include the use of whitespace, font, color, imagery, and navigation. Setting objectives, drafting wireframes, developing visuals, doing user testing, and working with developers are all steps in the process of putting the minimalist design into practice. Following the launch, continuous maintenance and observation guarantee that the design is still applicable and efficient.

CHAPTER IV

Choosing Essential Technology

Identifying essential vs. non-essential technology
One of the most essential skills in managing the increasingly complicated world of digital tools and services available today is the ability to distinguish between vital and non-essential technologies. The term "essential technology" refers to the apparatus and programs that are necessary for accomplishing individual or group objectives, raising efficiency, and facilitating day-to-day activities. These technologies usually fulfill essential roles and are required to keep efficiency and competitiveness high. On the other side, non-essential technology refers to devices or services that might offer extra features or comforts but are not necessary for primary goals or operations. It takes a sophisticated grasp of demands, goals, and the possible effects of each technology on overall performance and success to distinguish between non-essential and essential technology.

When defining necessary technology in a personal setting, the focus is frequently on instruments and gadgets that facilitate daily activities, communication, and self-organization. For example, a lot of people now consider smartphones to be indispensable as they act as a central location for productivity apps, communication, and information access. In a similar vein, laptops and personal computers are essential for work, school, and play. People can use these gadgets to manage their personal money and calendars, communicate effectively, and access necessary applications. Another example of an essential technological advancement is cloud storage services like

Dropbox or Google Drive, which offer safe and convenient storage for private files, images, and other digital assets.

Depending on the business and unique organizational requirements, several technologies are required in professional contexts. CRM software, email, and instant messaging platforms, enterprise resource planning (ERP) systems, and other communication tools are examples of core technologies. The data management, customer contacts, and internal processes that are necessary for operational effectiveness and corporate expansion are made more accessible by these technologies. Because of legal restrictions and the vital nature of the services offered, specialized software for patient management or financial analysis may be deemed necessary in sectors like healthcare and finance.

The line separating necessary technology from non-necessary technology is not always sharp and may alter over time as organizational requirements and technological advancements change. What is needed now might not be essential tomorrow or become antiquated, requiring constant assessment and adjustment. Furthermore, opinions about what constitutes critical technology can be influenced by both business culture and personal tastes. While stability and dependability may take precedence over embracing the newest trends, other firms may prioritize investing in state-of-the-art technology in order to preserve a competitive edge.

Technology that is not necessary for basic operations but offers extra features or conveniences falls into the category of non-essential technology. These technologies frequently improve productivity, inventiveness, or user experience without having an immediate effect on core corporate operations. Examples include cutting-edge yet unnecessary gadgets and equipment, specialist software for specialized tasks, and project management systems with advanced collaborative features. The adoption and usage of these technologies should be assessed in light of their alignment with strategic goals and return on investment, even though they can provide advantages like better workflow or increased creativity.

The process of determining which technology is non-essential entails determining if the extra features or conveniences are worth the money, effort, and resources needed for setup and upkeep. For example, even if a new project management tool has sophisticated features for task tracking and team collaboration, its adoption might not be warranted if current solutions are sufficient to meet organizational needs. Similarly, acquiring the newest consumer electronics or wearable technology could be innovative or enjoyable for the individual, but it might not have a significant impact on productivity or vital corporate goals.

Differentiating between necessary and non-necessary technologies in both personal and professional settings calls for a methodical approach. This entails assessing how the deployment of technology will affect specific needs, objectives, and workflows. Finding any gaps or inefficiencies that critical technology can solve is made more accessible by carrying out a thorough needs assessment. Understanding user needs and preferences is also made possible by stakeholder participation and feedback, which helps to guarantee that technology investments are in line with corporate priorities and strategic goals.

An important factor in deciding whether technology is necessary or not is cost-benefit analysis. Investments in essential technology usually pay for themselves in a clear and quantifiable way, such as increased compctitive advantage, better service delivery, or increased efficiency. Even though they provide extra features or conveniences, non-essential technology investments could not offer as noticeable or quick of a return on investment. Companies and individuals need to carefully consider these aspects in order to decide how best to prioritize their technology expenditures and where to focus their resources.

The identification of vital technologies also involves taking strategic alignment into account. Essential technologies assist both strategic initiatives and basic business functions by being tightly aligned with organizational goals and priorities. Investing in cybersecurity solutions, for instance, might be crucial for safeguarding private information and upholding legal compliance in sectors like healthcare and banking. Non-essential technology, on the other hand, can be more in line with departmental aims or personal preferences than with overarching company goals.

Assessing risk and technological dependency are crucial aspects to take into account when deciding which technology is required or not. Reliance on specific technology for essential functions may lead to weaknesses, like dangers related to cybersecurity or disruptions in operations in case of system malfunctions or outages. Companies need to evaluate the possible consequences of technology malfunctions and create backup plans to reduce the risks related to critical technologies. Even while non-essential technologies present less operational risk, it is still important to consider how they will affect the overall resilience and flexibility of the company.

To sum up, distinguishing between technology that is necessary and that which does not necessitate a sophisticated comprehension of the requirements, priorities, and strategic goals of both individuals and organizations. Tools and systems that are essential to accomplishing main objectives, increasing productivity, and facilitating day-to-day operations are included in the category of critical technology. Additional features or conveniences that could improve productivity or user experience but are not necessary for core business operations are considered non-essential technology. Through comprehensive requirements assessments, cost-benefit analyses, and risk assessments, individuals and organizations can make well-informed decisions regarding resource allocation and technology investment prioritization.

Tools and devices for a minimalist tech setup

The selection of tools and gadgets in the quest for a minimalist tech setup is critical to increasing productivity, reducing distractions, and encouraging a healthy digital lifestyle. This section examines numerous gadgets and tools that fit nicely into a minimalist tech setup, emphasizing the devices' adaptability, functionality, and compliance with the ideas of digital minimalism.

Desktop and laptop computers are essential components of any tech setup, and selecting the appropriate one can have a significant influence on digital wellbeing and productivity. Choosing a gadget that balances simplicity and performance is essential for a minimalist approach. Popular alternatives include devices like the MacBook Air and Dell XPS series because of their powerful performance, elegant appearance, and lightweight nature. These gadgets are adaptable choices for a minimalist digital setup since they can handle a broad range of jobs, from simple productivity to more difficult creative work.

Because of their portability and flexibility, tablets and convertible laptops are perfect for a minimalist digital setup. Products such as the Microsoft Surface Pro and iPad Pro combine the portability of a computer with the capability of a tablet, enabling users to transition between traditional keyboard input and touch-based interaction. Compared to conventional notebooks or desktops, these devices offer a more tactile and immersive experience, making them especially helpful for note-taking, reading, and leisurely surfing.

For those who emphasize reading and learning, digital minimalist e-readers like the Kindle or Kobo are indispensable tools. These gadgets, which have e-ink displays that simulate the appearance of ink on paper, provide a distraction-free reading experience. For voracious readers who wish to cut back on their use of real books and eliminate internet distractions, e-readers are the perfect option because they are portable, lightweight, and have a long battery life.

Although smartphones are a common sight in modern life, selecting a gadget that encourages awareness and concentration is crucial for a minimalist digital setup. Devices like the iPhone SE and the Google Pixel series put performance and essential functions ahead of ostentatious embellishments. These smartphones are dependable instruments for communication, productivity, and entertainment without overburdening users with features and notifications because of their excellent cameras, effective processors, and lengthy battery lives.

For minimalist tech settings, digital note-taking devices such as the iPad Pro with Apple Pencil or the reMarkable tablet are invaluable resources. With the help of these gadgets, users may digitally sketch ideas, mark documents, and take handwritten notes, simulating paper without the mess of actual notebooks and paper. The seamless integration of digital note-taking devices with cloud services facilitates note organization and access across devices, hence augmenting productivity and mitigating the necessity for physical clutter.

Wireless mice and keyboards are necessary add-ons for a minimalist computer setup since they improve ergonomic comfort and create a clutter-free workstation. Modern workstations are complemented by devices that offer silent, responsive typing experiences, such as the Apple Magic Keyboard or the Logitech MX Keys. With its precise cursor control and programmable buttons, wireless mice— like the Logitech MX Master series and Apple Magic Mouse —are adaptable instruments for creativity and productivity.

Adding external monitors to minimalist tech sets is an excellent idea because they provide you with more screen real estate for multitasking and creative work. High-resolution screens with excellent color reproduction are provided by monitors such as the LG UltraFine displays and the Dell UltraSharp series, which improve the visual experience for applications like data processing, photo editing, and video production. By combining external displays with laptops or desktop computers, a dual-screen configuration can be achieved that enhances productivity and workflow efficiency while keeping the workplace uncluttered.

Practical additions for a minimalist tech setup, wireless chargers, and docking stations clear up cord clutter and streamline device management. Fast charging capabilities and stylish designs come together in products like the Belkin Boost Up Wireless Charging Pad and Twelve South HiRise Duet, which let users charge several devices at once without tangles of cables. With the extra ports and connectivity choices that docking stations, like the CalDigit TS3 Plus or OWC Thunderbolt Dock, offer, users can easily attach peripherals, external drives, and monitors.

A minimalist tech setup might benefit from the added convenience and functionality of smart home appliances like voice assistants and smart speakers. Voice commands may be used to control entertainment systems, lighting, and temperature thanks to devices like the Google Nest Hub and Amazon Echo, which interact smoothly with other smart home services and products. In addition, these gadgets can act as digital assistants, handling calendars, sending reminders, and responding to inquiries without the need for further screens or gadgets.

For those who value attention and concentration, digital minimalists need noise-canceling headphones. Superior noise cancellation technology is available in devices such as the Bose QuietComfort line and the Sony WH-1000XM4, which reduce background noise and improve audiobooks, podcasts, and music listening in noisy surroundings. These headphones are perfect for travel, work, and play without the need for cumbersome gear because they are lightweight, comfy, and portable.

To ensure data protection and accessibility while keeping a minimal tech setup, cloud storage and backup options are necessary. Users may save, sync, and share files across different platforms with the help of services like Google Drive, Dropbox, or iCloud, which offer seamless connections with devices and applications. Cloud backup services, like Carbonite or Backblaze, offer automated data backups to guard against data loss from theft, device failure, and other unanticipated events.

Software and apps with a minimalist design are essential for keeping a digital workspace clear of clutter and increasing productivity. Apps that help users prioritize and efficiently manage their workload, such as Todoist and Things, provide users with easy-to-use interfaces for managing tasks and projects. Productivity apps, like Evernote or Notion, offer customizable note-taking and collaboration functionalities that facilitate ideation, content creation, and seamless cross-device sharing. With a minimal tech setup, these apps and software solutions are meant to maximize productivity and optimize workflows while reducing distractions.

For online privacy and security-conscious digital minimalists, virtual private networks (VPNs) are indispensable resources. By providing encrypted connections and anonymous browsing, services like ExpressVPN, NordVPN, and CyberGhost shield customers' data from hackers, advertisements, and governmental surveillance. By enabling users to access geo-restricted websites and content, VPNs improve online privacy and security without sacrificing user experience.

To sum up, creating a minimalist tech setup entails picking tools and gadgets with an emphasis on efficiency, simplicity, and functionality. Everything from laptops and cellphones to digital notepads and smart home appliances is essential for increasing productivity, reducing distractions, and encouraging a healthy digital lifestyle. Users can have a healthy connection with technology, optimize processes, and create a clutter-free workspace by selecting devices and accessories that adhere to the principles of digital minimalism. Adopting minimalist tools and gadgets will be more crucial as technology develops in the future to promote focus, creativity, and wellbeing in the digital era.

Strategies for mindful consumption of digital content

The consumption of digital information has become an essential aspect of many people's everyday lives worldwide in the current digital era. The availability and accessibility of digital content are unparalleled, ranging from news sections and social media updates to streaming movies and videos. While there are many advantages to digital content, like connectivity, education, and entertainment, there are drawbacks as well. Information overload, distraction, and even detrimental effects on mental health can result from its vast volume and frequent availability. Therefore, in order to preserve a healthy balance and optimize the advantages of technology while limiting any potential downsides, it is imperative to establish ways for conscious consumption of digital content.

Putting conscious limitations and bounds on digital content consumption is a valuable tactic. This entails choosing how much time and effort to devote to consuming digital content every day on a conscious basis. For example, people can choose particular time slots for viewing films, reading news online, and checking social media. By setting limits, people can avoid overindulging, lower their chance of becoming distracted, and make time for other activities that enhance wellbeing, like hobbies, physical activity, and quality time with loved ones.

Developing awareness of one's digital habits and their effects is another crucial tactic. This entails being aware of the reasons behind the use of digital content. People can consider, for instance, if they use social media to pass the time mindlessly, to stay in touch with friends and family, or to seek approval. People can choose when and how to interact with digital content more purposefully and in a way that is consistent with their beliefs and goals by being aware of their own motives and consumption patterns.

Mindful consumption of digital content can potentially benefit from mindfulness practices. Being cautious, which is focusing on the here and now without passing judgment, might assist people in being more conscious of the feelings, ideas, and actions associated with their use of digital devices. When interacting with digital content, one can create a sense of presence and awareness by using techniques like body scanning, mindful breathing, or meditation. People can improve focus, lessen impulsivity, and make thoughtful decisions about how to use digital devices and absorb content by engaging in mindfulness practices.

Making a digital space conducive to attentive consumption is another successful tactic. This involves designing digital environments to reduce distractions and encourage constructive communication. People can arrange their desktops, programs, and bookmarks, for instance, to maximize valuable tools and resources and reduce clutter and pointless alerts. Furthermore, limiting the amount of time spent on distracting websites with browser extensions or ad blockers might help you stay focused and lessen the urge to use technology excessively.

Another way to encourage mindfulness is to use digital content actively rather than passively. Selecting and interacting with content that is in line with one's interests, values, and objectives is known as active consuming. People can, for example, decide to follow content producers and sites that offer insightful and helpful content instead of ones that encourage negativity or comparison. Through the deliberate pursuit of educational and enlightening content, people can use digital platforms as instruments for their own development and education.

Another helpful tactic for mindful consumption is to have clear objectives and intents for your internet usage. This entails setting specific goals for utilizing digital devices and consuming content, such as keeping up with current affairs, picking up new skills, or making connections with people who share your interests. By establishing objectives, people can divert their attention from pointless browsing or scrolling and instead concentrate on things that enrich their lives. Maintaining a feeling of purpose and intentionality in digital consuming habits can be facilitated by routinely examining and modifying goals in light of shifting priorities.

Mindful consumption of digital content can also be supported by engaging in digital fasting or detoxification. This is setting aside time to contemplate, refuel, and reestablish connections with offline activities by purposefully stepping away from digital gadgets and content intake. People can, for instance, set out particular days or times every week to disconnect from email, social media, and other online resources. Digital detoxes provide people the chance to reestablish their connection with technology, lower their stress levels, and develop a more harmonious balance between their online and offline lives.

Gaining the ability to think critically is crucial for sifting through the large quantity of digital content that is out there and differentiating factual information from clickbait or false information. When recognizing information as accurate or genuine, critical thinking entails challenging presumptions, assessing the evidence, and taking into account many points of view. By confirming sources, fact-checking material, and exercising caution when it comes to stuff that lacks credibility or appears too good to be true, people can exercise critical thinking. People who are able to think critically are better able to choose the content they interact with and spread, which helps create a more responsible and considerate digital environment.

Creating a peer and mentor support network can also encourage thoughtful digital content consumption. This entails establishing connections with people who have similar beliefs and interests to your own in order to receive advice and help in making intelligent decisions regarding your use of digital media. People can work on projects that support their objectives and aspirations, share resources, and communicate ideas by taking part in online communities, forums, or discussion groups. Creating a network of people who share your values helps support and strengthen good habits and mindful internet consumption.

Ultimately, mental and general well-being depend on striking a healthy balance between digital and offline activities. This entails placing a high value on in-person communication, physical activity, and self-care routines that ease tension and encourage relaxation. People can lessen their reliance on digital gadgets and create opportunities for meaningful connections and experiences by including offline activities in their daily routines. Maintaining a healthy perspective on technology's place in lives and making sure that digital consumption enhances rather than diminishes general well-being are made possible by striking a balance between digital and offline activities.

To sum up, developing mindful digital content consumption techniques is crucial to navigating the digital world with purpose, equilibrium, and wellbeing. People can minimize the adverse effects of technology while maximizing its positive aspects by establishing clear boundaries, increasing awareness, engaging in mindfulness practices, and fostering a positive online community. A good connection with digital devices and materials is encouraged by active consumption, goal-setting, and the use of digital detoxes. Increasing critical thinking abilities, creating a community of support, and striking a good balance between online and offline activities all help people use digital content in daily life in a more thoughtful and satisfying way.

CHAPTER V

Establishing Digital Boundaries

Setting boundaries for technology use

In the era of digitalization, where technology is ingrained in almost every facet of daily existence, establishing limits on technology use has grown in significance for preserving equilibrium, efficiency, and general welfare. Technology provides unmatched ease, connectivity, and information access. This includes cell phones, PCs, tablets, and other linked gadgets. But the allure of digital diversions and the availability of technology all the time can cause problems like information overload, lower productivity, and even detrimental effects on mental health. As a result, it's critical for people, families, and organizations to set conscious, unambiguous boundaries surrounding technology use.

Establishing precise times and locations for device usage is an essential part of establishing boundaries for technology use. People might set aside specific times during the day to check their emails, browse social media, or indulge in online amusement. People can concentrate on other concerns, like work, family time, exercise, or hobbies, without being constantly distracted by digital devices by setting out specified hours for technology use. Similar to this, designating specific areas of the house—like dining rooms or bedrooms—as device-free zones can improve in-person family interactions and encourage better sleep hygiene.

Restricting the use of technology during particular events or activities is another crucial boundary-setting tactic. People can set guidelines, for example, prohibiting the use of cellphones or social media during meetings, dinners, and family get-togethers. In addition to improving communication skills and encouraging more aware and present-minded social interactions, this exercise also lessens the tendency to multitask, which can lower the caliber of social interactions. By placing a higher value on in-person interactions than virtual diversion, people can fortify their bonds and enhance their general state of wellbeing.

Another helpful tactic for establishing limits on technology use is to introduce digital detoxification periods or days. Digital detoxes entail setting aside specific time to unplug from electronics and internet activities in order to rejuvenate, contemplate, and rekindle interest in non-digital activities. This technique can assist people in lowering their stress levels, getting better sleep, and regaining perspective on the place of technology in their lives. Weekends and holidays alike offer chances for people to disconnect from technology and partake in hobbies, outdoor pursuits, or artistic efforts without the incessant barrage of digital alerts and notifications.

Setting limits on technology use also entails skillfully handling warnings and notifications. There might be a constant barrage of interruptions and diversions due to the widespread use of digital devices and programs that transmit notifications for emails, messages, social media updates, and news alerts. By turning off unnecessary alerts, designating specific times to check messages, and giving priority to vital information, people can lessen the impact of notifications. People can reclaim control over their attention and concentrate on things that demand long-term focus and productivity by limiting their notifications.

Establishing standards for work-life balance is another aspect of setting boundaries for technology use, especially for those who work from home or remotely. The growing trend of telecommuting and flexible work schedules can cause a blurring of work and personal life, resulting in more extended workdays and higher levels of stress. People can designate particular work hours, set up distinct workstations, and build routines that divide work from personal time in order to preserve a healthy work-life balance. Setting these boundaries enables people to prioritize rest and relaxation during their free time and maintain productivity during work hours.

Establishing limits on technology use is essential for families and parents who want to support the healthy growth and wellbeing of their children and teenagers. In addition to limiting exposure to potentially hazardous content, setting rules and norms for screen time, internet usage, and online safety aids in the development of responsible digital habits in kids. To ensure age-appropriate content and safe online interactions, parents can monitor and supervise their children's online activity through the use of parental control settings on devices and applications. Parents may empower their children to make educated decisions about technology use and encourage healthy screen time habits by establishing boundaries at an early age.

Establishing limits on technology use in classrooms is crucial for creating a positive learning atmosphere and encouraging student achievement. Guidelines for the use of digital devices in the school can be created by educators and teachers. For example, specific hours can be set aside for utilizing computers, tablets, or smartphones for assignments, research, and teamwork. Teachers can also instruct kids in responsible online conduct, digital citizenship, and the value of striking a balance between online and offline activities. Teachers can establish a productive and happy learning environment that encourages student participation and achievement by establishing clear expectations and boundaries.

Establishing limits on technology use in the workplace is crucial for encouraging employee productivity, teamwork, and work-life balance. Employers can set rules and regulations around the use of email, digital devices, and communication tools during working hours to make sure that technology improves worker performance and wellbeing rather than hinders it. Offering employees with training and resources on how to prioritize tasks, control digital distractions, and use technology effectively can help them stay focused and accomplish their career objectives. Employers may create a happy work environment and lower employee burnout by encouraging a good work-life balance.

Digital self-regulation and mindfulness are viable approaches to establishing limits on technology use. Digital mindfulness entails making deliberate decisions about how and when to use digital devices, being conscious of one's digital habits, and understanding the impact of technology on mental and emotional health. Methods like breathing exercises, time management techniques, and mindfulness meditation can help people become more self-aware, less stressed, and more focused in the face of digital distractions. People can improve their capacity to establish and uphold boundaries for technology use, which will increase their productivity and overall wellbeing, by engaging in digital mindfulness practices.

Establishing boundaries for technology use and promoting healthy digital habits can also be accomplished by setting up an accountability system and support network. People can ask friends, relatives, or coworkers who have similar objectives to manage technology use and preserve work-life balance for support. Achieving digital boundaries and goals can be aided by mutual agreements or check-ins with accountability partners, which can offer support, inspiration, and feedback on progress. People can develop resilience, maintain accountability, and maintain healthy habits for regulating technology use in daily life by working together with others.

In the end, establishing limits on technology use is about intentionally controlling how digital gadgets and content affect daily activities, interpersonal connections, and general wellbeing. People can cultivate better tech habits and attitudes by setting deliberate boundaries, designating areas accessible of electronics, engaging in digital detoxes, controlling alerts, and encouraging a work-life balance. Setting limits on technology use enables people to prioritize essential activities, make well-informed decisions, and lead balanced, satisfying lives in the digital age—whether at work, home, school, or in their personal lives.

Creating a minimalist digital workspace

The process of creating a minimalist digital workstation includes planning a neat, clutter-free space that encourages concentration, output, and creativity. The idea of minimalism has expanded to encompass digital settings in the digital age, where technology is an integral part of daily life and work. A digital workspace that is minimalistic prioritizes efficiency, intentionality, and simplicity. This helps people to improve their relationship with technology, minimize distractions, and expedite operations.

Decluttering and organizing digital files, papers, and programs is the foundation of a minimalist digital workspace. Digital clutter can overwhelm and reduce productivity, just as physical clutter can cause visual and mental distractions. Essential steps include naming conventions that make sense, routinely purging superfluous files, and organizing data into properly designated folders. Cloud storage systems, like iCloud, Dropbox, and Google Drive, provide easy ways to save and retrieve data on multiple devices, decreasing the requirement for physical storage space and streamlining document administration.

Another critical component of designing a minimalist digital workstation is selecting the appropriate gear. Making the switch to a more compact system, such as a laptop in place of a desktop computer, can free up space and lessen visual clutter. Well-made, minimally bezel-adorned displays, along with ergonomic keyboards and mice, add to a tidy and cozy workstation. Wireless accessories can help reduce the amount of cables that are visible, and docking stations offer more connectivity possibilities without making things more complicated. A hardware selection that adheres to minimalist principles guarantees functionality without of superfluous features or complexity.

In a minimalist digital workstation, digital note-taking tools are essential and can take the place of traditional notebooks and paper. Without the need for physical clutter, devices like the reMarkable tablet and the iPad Pro with Apple Pencil provide a paper-like experience for taking notes, scribbling ideas, and annotating documents. Users can access and manage notes across devices thanks to these products' seamless integration with cloud services. People can simplify organizing, cut down on paper waste, and increase productivity in a minimalist workspace by digitizing note-taking.

Maintaining a neat and effective digital workstation requires using a minimalist approach to software and applications. People can build a minimalist desktop by grouping necessary apps onto a dock or taskbar rather than overcrowding the desktop with icons and shortcuts. Task management, note-taking, and project collaboration can be streamlined in a clutter-free environment by using productivity tools like Todoist, Evernote, or Notion. Reducing the amount of installed applications enhances concentration on critical work and lessens digital distractions.

Adopting a distraction-free writing environment is another aspect of embracing a minimalist digital office. Text editors with simple interfaces that do away with menus, toolbars, and notifications include FocusWriter, Writemonkey, and iA Writer. These programs help people concentrate only on writing, which boosts productivity and creativity. Distraction-free writing tools reduce visual clutter and superfluous features to provide a calm, concentrated workspace that is ideal for generating excellent work.

For efficient workflow organization and task prioritization, a minimalist digital workspace must incorporate productivity and task management tools. Simple interfaces are offered by platforms like Asana, Microsoft

To-Do, Trello, and others for organizing and tracking tasks, projects, and due dates. With the help of these technologies, people can monitor progress, see workflows, and work together with others in a clutter-free setting. People can decrease mental clutter, enhance time management, and increase productivity in their digital workspace by centralizing task management.

In a minimalist digital workspace, where preserving sensitive data is balanced with streamlined workflows and effective organization, maintaining digital security and privacy is crucial. Data can be protected from cyber threats and illegal access by utilizing secure cloud storage solutions, creating strong passwords, and turning on two-factor authentication. Tools and browser extensions that promote privacy, such as DuckDuckGo for internet searches and Signal for texting, offer options that prioritize user privacy without sacrificing functionality. People may design a simple, safe, and secure digital workspace by putting security and privacy first.

Optimizing the digital workspace to enhance focus and concentration is another aspect of designing a minimalist digital workspace. White noise applications, ambient sound generators, and noise-canceling headphones are a few examples of tools that can reduce distractions and foster a calm, productive environment. By encouraging awareness and lowering mental clutter, digital mindfulness and time management methods like the Pomodoro Technique or mindful breathing exercises can improve attention and productivity. People can maintain a balanced and thoughtful attitude to digital work by implementing these tools and strategies into their everyday routines.

Promoting physical comfort and well-being in a minimalist digital workstation requires the integration of ergonomic furniture and accessories. Ergonomic seats, monitor stands, and adjustable standing desks all assist people in maintaining good posture and lower their chance of pain or injury when using computers for extended periods of time. Tangled cords are avoided with cable management tools like cable trays and clamps, which also help to keep a workspace tidy. It is possible for people to build a minimalist digital workstation that promotes both productivity and wellness by giving ergonomic design first priority.

A minimalist digital workspace must have communication and collaboration tools in order for people to effectively connect and work with clients, coworkers, or collaborators. Slack, Zoom, and Microsoft Teams are a few examples of platforms that offer simple, clutter-free interfaces for video conferencing, project collaboration, and messaging. Through the centralization of communication and collaboration technologies, individuals can enhance team productivity, minimize digital clutter, and streamline workflows. By incorporating these technologies into a simple digital workstation, you can maintain a neat and orderly atmosphere while encouraging effective communication and teamwork.

It takes constant upkeep and assessment to keep a minimalist digital workstation functional and guarantee that operations stay effective. Consistently evaluating digital data, apps, and workflows makes it easier to see areas where procedures may be made simpler, duplication can be removed, and productivity can be increased. A neat and effective digital workspace is facilitated by cleaning digital equipment, organizing digital information, and updating software. People may design a digital workspace that promotes attention, productivity, and well-being in the digital age by embracing simplicity and adopting a minimalist attitude.

Managing notifications and interruptions

Keeping track of alerts and distractions has become essential in the digital age of constant technology, as it affects concentration, output, and overall health. Notifications function as alerts for incoming messages, updates, reminders, and notifications from apps and services, and they can originate from computers, cell phones, or other linked devices. Notifications can help spread important information and promote communication, but they can also cause distraction, lower productivity, and more stress than they should. Therefore, maximizing digital workflows, reducing distractions, and promoting a positive connection with technology all depend on efficiently managing notifications and interruptions.

Prioritizing and adjusting notification settings according to relevance and importance is a crucial tactic for handling interruptions and notifications. Users can personalize their notification choices on the majority of devices and applications. This includes selecting which notifications to receive, changing the tone of the notifications, and establishing priority levels. People can cut down on pointless distractions and concentrate on vital tasks and activities by giving priority to notifications from essential contacts, projects that require immediate attention, and time-sensitive information. By personalizing notification preferences, you can make sure that notifications are helpful without overloading the user with unnecessary details.

Setting up designated times to check for and reply to notifications is another intelligent tactic, as opposed to letting them constantly disrupt work. Through the process of batching messages into specific time intervals throughout the day, people can reduce distractions and focus during focused work times. To stay connected and maintain unbroken times of concentrated work, people can set aside 15 to 20 minutes at the start or end of each hour to examine and reply to messages and alerts. Because batching notifications lessens the cognitive load brought on by frequent interruptions, it encourages effective time management and boosts productivity.

Putting in place a notification hierarchy is another innovative way to efficiently handle alerts and disruptions. Similar to an emergency response triage system, a notification hierarchy divides notifications into tiers of relevance and urgency. Notifications deemed high-priority, including urgent communications from coworkers or crucial system alarms, are given precedence for prompt notice and action. Notifications with a medium priority, such as updates and non-urgent messages, are frequently examined during scheduled breaks or downtime. To reduce distraction and preserve attention, low-priority notifications—like social network updates or advertising messages—are either disabled or filtered. People can handle incoming alerts according to their respective relevance and productivity impact by creating a notification hierarchy.

The process of efficiently managing alerts can be streamlined by utilizing the tools and features that operating systems and applications offer for this purpose. Many platforms and devices have features like "Do Not Disturb" mode, which temporarily turns off alerts at certain times or occasions, like bedtime or meetings. Users can also regulate when and how notifications appear by using features like notification badges, snooze options, and notification filters. Through the use of these tools, users may customize notification settings to suit their tastes and workflow, making sure that alerts complement daily activities rather than interfere with them.

People can also learn to better handle notifications and interruptions by engaging in digital mindfulness practices and purposeful technology use. Being conscious of one's digital habits, such as when and how to respond to notifications, entails being in the moment. Methods like mindful breathing, meditation, and time management techniques can assist people in staying focused and lessening the influence of electronic distractions. People can become conscious of their notification patterns and intentionally choose whether to interact with alerts and when to prioritize undisturbed work time by engaging in digital mindfulness practices.

In the digital age, keeping a distraction-free workstation is crucial to reducing disruptions and preserving productivity. Setting aside particular locations or times for concentrated work—free from notifications and other distractions—can aid in improving focus and productivity. For instance, people can reduce outside distractions and establish a productive environment by using designated workstations, such as quiet rooms or home offices. Clear boundaries and expectations should also be communicated to coworkers and family members in order to minimize disruptions and promote concentrated work periods. People can improve their digital processes, lower stress levels, and improve concentration by setting up a distraction-free workstation.

Another smart way to handle notifications and disruptions in the digital era is to set limits on communication and technology use. Setting rules on when and how to communicate with family, clients, and coworkers enables people to strike a balance between being responsive and having undisturbed work time. Establishing defined office hours or response times for emails and messages, for instance, clarifies expectations and enables people to better handle incoming communications. Additionally, you can let people know when you're unavailable and lessen the need to answer right away by utilizing automatic responses and out-of-office messages during concentrated work sessions. One way for people to prioritize focused work time and keep lines of communication open with others is to set boundaries for technology use.

Effective interruption management requires engaging with notifications and communicating mindfully. Rather than responding without thinking, people might engage in mindful engagement by considering the significance and applicability of each warning before acting. People can effectively handle alerts by using strategies like the "two-minute rule," which suggests tackling short chores right away or putting off big ones for later consideration. Furthermore, making time for in-depth work and uninterrupted concentration windows enables people to interact with alerts carefully and react appropriately when called upon. Individuals can lessen the effects of disruptions and preserve productivity in their digital workflows by engaging in mindful communication practices.

By putting in place both digital and physical barriers to distractions, people can better control their alerts and stay focused on essential tasks. Physical barriers indicate to others that having undisturbed work time is necessary. Examples of these barriers include shutting doors, wearing noise-canceling headphones, and hanging a "Do Not Disturb" sign. Digital barriers reduce distractions and facilitate focused work sessions. Examples of these barriers include turning off pop-up warnings, muting unnecessary messages, and utilizing focus mode on devices and apps. People may design a workspace that encourages productivity, creativity, and well-being in the digital age by erecting barriers to disruptions.

Developing a respectful and aware culture in teamwork and communication can also help with efficiently handling alerts and disruptions. Prioritizing and streamlining information flow in team environments can be achieved by creating conventions and procedures for communication, such as using email for non-urgent questions and instant messaging for urgent ones. Respecting set work hours and response windows from coworkers helps to maintain concentrated work sessions and lowers the number of interruptions. Furthermore, engaging in intelligent communication and active listening can reduce the need for follow-up communications and interruptions, which can enhance productivity and efficiency in group settings. Teams may reduce disruptions in their digital workflows and maximize communication practices by cultivating a culture of mindfulness and respect.

Last but not least, maintaining optimal productivity and proficiently handling disruptions requires routinely reviewing and modifying notification settings and tactics. Reviewing notification settings, workflow patterns, and reaction times on a regular basis enables people to spot problem areas and implement the required fixes. People can find what best suits their specific tastes and work styles by experimenting with various notification management systems, strategies, and timetables. Through constant assessment and improvement of notification tactics, people can stay focused, lower their stress levels, and be more productive in their digital workflows.

In summary, sound notification and interruption management is essential for preserving concentration, output, and wellbeing in the digital age. People can minimize distractions and improve their digital workflows by prioritizing and personalizing notification settings, setting aside particular times to check for and respond to alerts, and putting notification hierarchies in place. Utilizing digital mindfulness techniques, setting up distraction-free work areas, and utilizing notification management tools can all help to promote focused work sessions and reduce disruptions. Establishing limits on technological use, encouraging thoughtful communication, and erecting barriers to disruptions all assist people in efficiently handling notifications and preserving productivity. People can improve their digital workflows, lower their stress levels, and find a better work-life balance by routinely reviewing and modifying their notification tactics.

Strategies for balancing online and offline time

Finding a balance between online and offline time has grown more difficult in the digital era, but it is essential for preserving both physical and mental health. The ubiquitous presence of technology, encompassing computers, tablets, smartphones, and other linked gadgets, has transformed people's social, professional, and interaction patterns. Digital tools and the internet have many advantages, like increased productivity, social isolation, and reduced screen time and connectivity. However, they can also cause problems like digital burnout and reduced productivity. Therefore, cultivating a positive relationship with technology and encouraging a well-rounded lifestyle requires establishing ways to strike a balance between online and outside time.

Creating daily routines with specific times allotted for both digital and offline activities is a valuable tactic for striking a balance between online and offline time. People can control their online presence without letting it take over their entire day by designating distinct times for utilizing digital gadgets, checking emails, and using social media. In a similar vein, scheduling time for offline pursuits like physical activity, hobbies, reading, or socializing with loved ones aids in helping people unplug from screens and emotionally and physically rejuvenate. Establishing a well-rounded daily schedule that includes both online and offline activities boosts wellbeing, encourages productivity, and lessens the adverse effects of excessive screen time.

An additional helpful tactic for striking a balance between online and offline time is to practice mindfulness and purposeful technology use. Being mindful entails being in the moment and conscious of one's feelings, ideas, and behaviors—including the use of technology and when it is employed. People can have more control over their digital habits and make deliberate decisions about when to use digital devices and when to unplug by engaging in mindful awareness practices. In order to foster a good balance between online and offline activities, people can benefit from practices like conscious breathing, meditation, and digital detoxes, which can enhance mental clarity, attention, and general wellbeing.

Establishing limits on technology use is essential for striking a balance between online and offline time and keeping a positive connection with gadgets. Setting limits on screen use before bed, during family get-togethers, or during meals can assist people in prioritizing in-person communication and offline activities. Additionally, focusing on work or leisure time without the continual interruption of digital messages is supported by utilizing features like "Do Not Disturb" mode, creating device-free zones in the home, and arranging times during the day without using technology. Establishing unambiguous guidelines for using technology can help people stay focused, sleep better, and feel better overall.

Maintaining a healthy lifestyle and striking a balance between online and offline time can be achieved through physical activity and outdoor sports. Sports, outdoor recreation, and exercise not only improve physical health but also inspire people to get outside and interact with nature instead of sullying themselves with screens. Engaging in physical activities such as walking, yoga, or sports can help people decompress, lower stress levels, and elevate their mood without being constantly stimulated by electronics. Regular physical activity helps people maintain a balanced lifestyle and lessen the harmful effects of excessive screen time. It can be incorporated into daily routines.

In order to balance time spent online and offline and to promote general wellbeing, it is crucial to cultivate meaningful interactions and social connections offline. Bonds are strengthened and dependency on digital communication is decreased when spending quality time with family, friends, and loved ones through in-person interactions, shared activities, and meaningful talks. Online platforms are unable to entirely replace the emotional support, empathy, and connection that offline social encounters offer. Through fostering social connections and offline relationships, people can cultivate a feeling of community and belonging in their lives, as well as maintain a balanced attitude to technology use.

Resetting one's relationship with technology and striking a balance between online and offline time can be accomplished through the use of digital detoxes and technology-free periods. Digital detoxes entail setting aside specific time to unplug from electronics and internet activities in order to rest, think, and pursue hobbies offline. Digital detoxes, which might take the form of a weekend away from smartphones, an evening without displays, or a trip without technology, offer chances to detach from the never-ending demands of digital devices and re-establish a connection with the natural world and oneself. People can minimize their screen usage, ease their digital tiredness, and bring back balance to their lives by routinely engaging in digital detoxes.

Another helpful tactic for striking a balance between online and offline time and promoting personal development and contentment is to take up creative and offline activities. Outside of digital contexts, hobbies like painting, gardening, cooking, creating, or playing an instrument provide possibilities for creativity, self-expression, and relaxation. Taking up creative activities enables people to detach from screens, lower their stress levels, and develop new interests and abilities that enhance their overall wellbeing. People can lead balanced lives and have positive relationships with technology by making time for offline and creative activities.

To balance online and offline time and support children's and teenagers' healthy development, it is crucial to promote digital well-being and responsible technology use within families and communities. Healthy digital habits are encouraged from an early age by teaching kids the value of digital balance, limiting screen time, and creating technology-free areas and times at home. In addition, setting an example of responsible technology use and spending time offline with your family fosters social interactions, communication skills, and quality time that all contribute to overall wellbeing. Families and communities can promote healthy growth and uphold a balanced approach to online and offline activities by placing a high priority on digital well-being and responsible technology use.

In order to balance online and offline time, maximize productivity, and maintain wellbeing, it is imperative to develop time management skills and prioritize activities properly. Setting objectives, ranking assignments, and scheduling time for both online and offline activities are all part of efficient time management. Methods like time blocking, the Pomodoro Technique, and making daily or weekly plans assist people in effectively managing their time and striking a balance between work, personal, and digital obligations. People may decrease procrastination, increase productivity, and strike a healthy balance between online and offline activities by mastering the skill of time management.

To balance online and offline time and make wise technology use decisions, it is critical to consider and assess one's digital habits and their effects on wellbeing.

By evaluating screen time, digital interactions, and offline experiences, people can find areas for growth and make changes to attain a more balanced lifestyle. Self-assessment tools, journaling, and mindfulness exercises are some of the techniques that might help with introspection and raise awareness of one's own tech-using behaviors. People can create strategies for attaining a balanced approach to online and offline activities and increasing general well-being by thinking critically about their digital habits and the effects they have on their lives.

In the end, striking a balance between online and offline time necessitates awareness, attention, and a dedication to digital age wellbeing. People can maintain a balanced lifestyle and maximize their well-being by creating daily routines, defining boundaries for technology use, participating in offline and offline activities, cultivating meaningful relationships offline, doing digital detoxes, and taking up creative hobbies. Finding a good balance between online and offline time requires fostering digital well-being in families and communities, learning time management techniques, and thinking critically about one's own digital habits. People may meet the demands of the digital age and lead satisfying, balanced lives by putting personal well-being first and putting these techniques into practice.

CONCLUSION

We've gone over the key ideas and strategies in "The Digital Minimalist's Handbook: A Guide to Simplifying Your Tech Life and Maximizing Productivity," which might assist you in taking back authority over your digital life. Even while the digital age is full of opportunities, we are frequently overloaded with constant notifications, never-ending information streams, and constant contact. You will find the methods and resources in this manual to help you go across this terrain with clarity and intention.

Beyond simply cutting back on screen time, digital minimalism promotes a thoughtful relationship with technology. You may make your digital interactions meaningful and enriching rather than draining from your life by adopting this mentality. We've looked at doable strategies for controlling alerts, establishing limits, and designing simple digital workspaces. These techniques aim to improve concentration, lessen distractions, and increase output.

This book's case studies demonstrate the significant effects that digital minimalism may have on wellbeing and productivity. These practical illustrations show how cutting back on technology may significantly enhance your productivity, mental clarity, and sense of well-being. You may create a more mindful and contented existence by putting the strategies in this handbook into practice and striking a healthier balance between your online and offline lives.

Keep in mind that the path to digital minimalism is a continuous one as you proceed. Make sure your digital behaviors are in line with your values and objectives by regularly evaluating and making adjustments. Embracing intentionality and simplicity in your electronic life opens doors to increased creativity, stronger relationships, and a more purposeful, productive life.

We appreciate you taking us on this journey with "The Digital Minimalist's Handbook." I hope the ideas and methods presented on these pages help you develop a more purposeful, productive, and balanced relationship with technology so you can prosper in the digital age.

Thank you for buying and reading/ listening to our book. If you found this book useful/ helpful please take a few minutes and leave a review on the platform where you purchased our book. Your feedback matters greatly to us.